Principals of Criminal Law

Law School Notes

2018

FitchLaw, Inc.

Copyright:
Copyright 2018 FitchLaw. All rights reserved. No part of this publication may be stored in a retrieval system, transmitted, or reproduced in any way, including but not limited to photocopy, photographs, magnetic, or other record, without the prior agreement and written permission of the publisher.

The author and publisher have made their best efforts to prepare this book. The author and publisher make no representation or warranties of any kind with regards to the completeness or accuracy of the contents herein and accepts no liability of any kind, including but not limited to performance, merchantability, fitness for any particular purpose or any losses or damages of any kind caused or alleged to be caused directly or indirectly from this book.

Trademarks:
FitchLaw Inc., has attempted throughout this book to distinguish proprietary trademarks from descriptive terms by following the capitalization style used by the manufacturer.

Published by: FitchLaw Inc.

FitchLaw Inc., welcome corrections and comments on its documents. In addition to comments, please send comments on typographical, formatting, or other errors. Simply make a copy of the relevant page, mark the error, and send it to fitchlawupdates@gmail.com.

Books and testing materials are available at special quantity discounts to use as premiums and sales promotions, or for corporate training programs, as well as other educational programs.

Printed in the United States of America. No part of this work may be reproduced or transmitted in any form or by any means, electronic, manual, photocopying, recording, or by any information storage and retrieval systems, without prior written permission of the publisher.

ISBN-13: 978-1986192064 (paperback)

Contents

1 Overview — 6

2 Basic Principles of Criminal Law — 8
- 2.1 Introduction — 8
  - 2.1.1 Beyond a Reasonable Doubt: *Owens v. State* — 9
- 2.2 Principles of Punishment — 9
  - 2.2.1 Utilitarianism — 10
  - 2.2.2 Retributivism — 10
  - 2.2.3 Justifying Punishment — 11
    - 2.2.3.1 Retributive and Utilitarian Justifications for Punishment: *The Queen v. Dudley and Stephens* — 11
    - 2.2.3.2 Sentencing: *People v. Du* — 11
- 2.3 Proportionality of Punishment — 12
  - 2.3.1 General Principles — 12
  - 2.3.2 Constitutional Principles — 13
    - 2.3.2.1 Rape and Capital Punishment: *Coker v. Georgia* — 13
    - 2.3.2.2 Three Strikes: *Ewing v. California* — 13
- 2.4 Statutory Interpretation — 14
  - 2.4.1 The Legality Principle — 14
  - 2.4.2 Crime without Law: *Commonwealth v. Mochan* — 15
  - 2.4.3 Statutory Interpretation and Institutional Competence: *Keeler v. Superior Court* — 15
  - 2.4.4 Statutory Clarity: *In re Banks* — 16
  - 2.4.5 Void for Vagueness: *City of Chicago v. Morales* — 16
  - 2.4.6 Interpreting Statutory Language: *Muscarello v. United States* — 17

3 Elements of a Crime — 18
- 3.1 Actus Reus — 18
  - 3.1.1 Voluntary vs. Involuntary Action: *Martin v. State* — 19
  - 3.1.2 Proving Involuntary Action: *State v. Utter* — 19
  - 3.1.3 Legal Duty to Act: *People v. Beardsley* — 19
  - 3.1.4 Failure to Act: *Barber v. Superior Court* — 20
  - 3.1.5 Constitutional Limitations on Criminalizing Conduct: *Lawrence v. Texas* — 20
- 3.2 Mens Rea — 21
  - 3.2.1 General Principles — 21
    - 3.2.1.1 General Culpability: *Regina v. Cunningham* — 21
    - 3.2.1.2 Transferred Intent: *People v. Conley* — 22
    - 3.2.1.3 Specific and General Intent — 22
    - 3.2.1.4 Common Law Specific Intent Crimes: BAFFLEPACK — 23
    - 3.2.1.5 MPC § 2.02: General Requirements of Culpability — 23

- 3.2.1.6 Knowledge of Attendant Circumstances and Willful Blindness ... 24
- 3.2.1.7 Defining Knowledge: *State v. Nations* ... 24
- 3.2.2 Strict Liability ... 25
  - 3.2.2.1 Public Welfare Offenses: *United States v. Cordoba-Hincapie* ... 25
  - 3.2.2.2 Inferring Mens Rea: *Staples v. United States* ... 25
  - 3.2.2.3 Legislative Silence as Strict Liability: *Garnett v. State* ... 26
- 3.2.3 Mistake and Mens Rea ... 27
  - 3.2.3.1 Common Law vs. MPC Mistake of Law and Fact ... 27
  - 3.2.3.2 Mistake of Fact: *People v. Navarro* ... 28
  - 3.2.3.3 Mistake of Law: *People v. Marrero* ... 29
  - 3.2.3.4 Unreasonable Mistake of Law: *Cheek v. United States* ... 29
- 3.3 Causation ... 30
  - 3.3.1 Actual Cause ... 32
    - 3.3.1.1 Acceleration: *Oxendine v. State* ... 32
  - 3.3.2 Proximate Cause ... 32
    - 3.3.2.1 Chain of Causation: *People v. Rideout* ... 32
    - 3.3.2.2 Superseding Intervening Cause: *Velazquez v. State* ... 33

4 Homicide   34
- 4.1 Common Law vs. Model Penal Code ... 34
- 4.2 Intentional Killing ... 35
  - 4.2.1 Murder ... 35
    - 4.2.1.1 Premeditation vs. Intent: *State v. Guthrie* ... 36
    - 4.2.1.2 Proving Premeditation: *Midgett v. State* ... 36
    - 4.2.1.3 Circumstantial Evidence of Premeditation: *State v. Forrest* ... 36
  - 4.2.2 Manslaughter ... 37
    - 4.2.2.1 Verbal Provocation: *Girouard v. State* ... 38
    - 4.2.2.2 Emotional Disturbance: *People v. Casassa* ... 39
  - 4.2.3 Unintentional Killing ... 39
    - 4.2.3.1 Implied Malice: *People v. Knoller* ... 40
    - 4.2.3.2 Proving Negligence: *State v. Hernandez* ... 40
    - 4.2.3.3 Omissions and Negligence: *State v. Williams* ... 41
  - 4.2.4 Felony-Murder ... 42
    - 4.2.4.1 Applying the Felony-Murder Rule: *People v. Fuller* ... 43
    - 4.2.4.2 Roth and Sundby, "The Felony-Murder Rule" ... 43
    - 4.2.4.3 Crump and Crump, "In Defense of the Felony-Murder Doctrine" ... 44
    - 4.2.4.4 Tomkovicz, "The Endurance of the Felony-Murder Rule" ... 44
    - 4.2.4.5 Inherently Dangerous Felonies: *People v. Howard* 44

		4.2.4.6	Independent Felony (or Merger) Limitation: *People v. Smith*	45
		4.2.4.7	Liability for a Non-Felon's Actions: *State v. Sophophone*	46
		4.2.4.8	Misdemeanor Manslaughter	47

5 Rape   48
5.1 Overview 48
    5.1.1   Annette Gordon Reed, *Celia's Case* 49
    5.1.2   C. Vann Woodward, Review of *Scottsboro: A Tragedy of the American South* 49
    5.1.3   NY Times Obituary for Ruth Schut 49
5.2 Forcible Rape 49
    5.2.1   The Force Requirement: *State v. Alston* 50
    5.2.2   Questioning the Force Requirement: *Rusk v. State* 50
    5.2.3   Removing the Force Requirement: *State v. Rusk* 51
    5.2.4   Susan Anger, *The Incident* 51
    5.2.5   Acquaintance Rape: *State of New Jersey in the Interest of M.T.S.* 51
    5.2.6   Ending Wife Rape: *People v. Liberta* 52
    5.2.7   Margaret Mitchell, *Gone With the Wind* 52
    5.2.8   Male Rape: *State v. Gounagias* 52
5.3 Mens Rea 52
    5.3.1   Mistake of Fact: *People v. Williams* 52
5.4 Statutory Rape 53
    5.4.1   *State v. Garnett* 54
    5.4.2   Equal Protection: *State v. Limon* 54

6 Defenses   55
6.1 Overview 55
6.2 Justification 55
    6.2.1   Self-Defense 56

		6.2.1.1	Self-Defense and Provocation: *United States v. Peterson*	57
		6.2.1.2	Self-Defense and Reasonable Belief: *People v. Goetz*	58
		6.2.1.3	Abused Spouse Syndrome: *State v. Norman* . .	58
		6.2.1.4	Imminence: *State v. Norman*	59
	6.2.2	Necessity		59
		6.2.2.1	MPC § 3.02 ("Choice of Evils") and ALI Commentary	60
		6.2.2.2	Emergencies: *Nelson v. State*	61
		6.2.2.3	Civil Disobedience: *United States v. Schoon* . .	61
		6.2.2.4	*The Queen v. Dudley and Stephens*	62

6.3 Excuse 62
    6.3.1   Duress 63

		6.3.1.1	Coercion to Smuggle Drugs: *United States v. Contento-Pachon*	64
		6.3.1.2	Duress and Murder: *People v. Anderson*	64
	6.3.2	Intoxication		65
		6.3.2.1	Specific Intent Crimes: *United States v. Veach*	65
	6.3.3	Insanity		66
		6.3.3.1	*United States v. Freeman*	66
		6.3.3.2	*State v. Johnson*	67
		6.3.3.3	Criminality and Wrongfulness: *State v. Wilson*	68
	6.3.4	Diminished Capacity		69
		6.3.4.1	*Clark v. Arizona*	70
	6.3.5	Infancy		71
		6.3.5.1	*In re Devon T*	71

7 Inchoate Offenses — 73

- 7.1 Overview — 73
- 7.2 Merger and Abandonment — 73
- 7.3 Attempt — 73
  - 7.3.1 General principles — 75
    - 7.3.1.1 Robbins, "Double Inchoate Crimes" — 75
    - 7.3.1.2 Ashworth, "Criminal Attempts and the Role of Resulting Harm under the Code, and in the Common Law" — 76
    - 7.3.1.3 ALI Comment to MPC § 5.05 — 77
  - 7.3.2 Mens Rea — 77
    - 7.3.2.1 Attempted Murder and Intent: *People v. Gentry* — 77
    - 7.3.2.2 Attempted Felony Murder: *Bruce v. State* — 78
  - 7.3.3 Actus Reus — 78
    - 7.3.3.1 *United States v. Mandujano* — 78
    - 7.3.3.2 Locus Poenitentiae: *Commonwealth v. Peaslee* — 79
    - 7.3.3.3 No Chance of Success: *People v. Rizzo* — 80
    - 7.3.3.4 *People v. Miller* — 80
    - 7.3.3.5 Preparation and Substantial Steps: *State v. Reeves* — 80
  - 7.3.4 Special defenses — 81
  - 7.3.5 Impossibility: *People v. Thousand* — 81
  - 7.3.6 Abandonment: *Commonwealth v. McCloskey* — 81
- 7.4 Assault — 82
- 7.5 Solicitation — 82
  - 7.5.1 Defining Solicitation: *State v. Mann* — 83
  - 7.5.2 Completed Communication: *State v. Cotton* — 83
- 7.6 Conspiracy — 83
  - 7.6.1 General Principles — 86
    - 7.6.1.1 Drug Smuggling: Kerman, *Orange is the New Black: My Year in a Women's Prison* — 86
    - 7.6.1.2 *People v. Carter* — 86
    - 7.6.1.3 Pinkerton Liability: *Pinkerton v. United States* — 87

- 7.6.2 *Mens rea* 87
  - 7.6.2.1 Conspiracy to Commit Implied Malice Murder: *People v. Swain* 87
  - 7.6.2.2 Suppliers as Conspirators: *People v. Lauria* ... 88
- 7.6.3 Actus Reus 89
  - 7.6.3.1 Goldstein, "Conspiracy to Defraud the United States" 89
  - 7.6.3.2 Inferring Conspiracy: *Commonwealth v. Azim* . 89
  - 7.6.3.3 *Commonwealth v. Cook* 90
- 7.6.4 Scope of the Agreement 90
  - 7.6.4.1 ALI Commentary to MPC § 5.03 90
  - 7.6.4.2 Wheel and Chain Conspiracies: *Kilgore v. State* 90
  - 7.6.4.3 Single Agreement, Multiple Offenses: *Braverman v. United States* 91
- 7.6.5 Defenses 91
  - 7.6.5.1 Wharton's Rule: *Ianelli v. United States* 91
  - 7.6.5.2 *Gebardi v. United States* 92
  - 7.6.5.3 Withdrawal from Conspiracy: *People v. Sconce* 93

8 Accomplice Liability   94

8.1 General Principles 95
- 8.1.1 Common Law Terminology: *State v. Ward* 95
- 8.1.2 Theoretical Foundations for Derivative Liability 96
- 8.1.3 *People v. Hoselton* 96
- 8.1.4 Kerman, *Orange is the New Black* 96

8.2 Mens Rea 96
- 8.2.1 *People v. Lauria* 96
- 8.2.2 No Principal, and Conduct vs. Result: *Riley v. State* .. 97
- 8.2.3 Natural-and-Probable Consequences Doctrine: *State v. Linscott* 97

8.3 Actus Reus 98
- 8.3.1 Slackjaw Deadeye: *State v. V.T.* 98
- 8.3.2 Small Encouragement: *Wilcox v. Jeffery* 98

8.4 Liability of Principals and Accomplices 99
- 8.4.1 Innocent Agency Doctrine: *Bailey v. Commonwealth* ... 99
- 8.4.2 Justification: *United States v. Lopez* 99
- 8.4.3 More Serious Crime than the Principal's: *People v. McCoy* 99

8.5 Limitations on Accomplice Liability 100
- 8.5.1 Aiding Your Own Victimization? *In re Megan R.* 100
- 8.5.2 Renunciation: *State v. Formella* 100

§ 1 Overview

1. Basic principles of criminal law.

   (a) Legality principle, reasonable doubt, retributivism, utilitarianism, sentencing, proportionality, institutional competency, statutory clarity, lenity.

2. Elements of a crime.

   (a) Actus reus: harm principle, conduct vs. status, omissions, duty, constitutional limitations.

   (b) Mens rea: culpability vs. elemental, specific intent vs. general intent, willful blindness, transferred intent, strict liability, public welfare offenses, mistake of fact, mistake of law, MPC subjectivity.

   (c) Causation: cause-in-fact, but-for, substantial factor, proximate cause, intervening acts.

3. Homicide.

   (a) Common law vs. MPC classifications, provocation (common law vs. MPC), implied malice/depraved heart, negligence, felony-murder rule, merger limitation, res gestae, misdemeanor manslaughter.

4. Rape.

   (a) Forcible rape: common law definition, forcible resistance requirement, threats, spouse exemption, apprehension of fear, acquaintance rape.

   (b) Mens rea: mistake of fact.

   (c) Statutory rape: policy goals, reforms, equal protection.

5. Defenses.

   (a) Failure of proof, offense modification, justification, excuse, noexculpatory public policy defense.

   (b) Justification: triggering conditions, necessity, proportionality.

      i. Self defense: common law vs. MPC, castle doctrine, immediacy vs. imminence, imperfect self-defense, abused spouse syndrome.

      ii. Necessity: MPC vs. common law, emergencies, civil disobedience

   (c) Excuse: theories (utilitarian, causation, character, free choice).

      i. Duress: coercion, immediacy, homicide.

      ii. Intoxication: voluntary vs. involuntary, specific intent crimes.

      iii. Insanity: deific decree, tests (right-wrong, M'Naghten, irresistible impulse, Durham/product, MPC/ALI).

iv. Diminished capacity: continuum of competence, mens rea variant vs. partial responsibility variant.

v. Infancy: under seven, seven to fourteen, above fourteen.

6. Inchoate offenses.

    (a) Rationales for punishment, law enforcement discretion.

    (b) Attempt: incomplete vs. complete, merger, conduct vs. results crimes, common law tests (first step, last step, physical proximity, dangerous proximity, indispensable element, probable desistance, abnormal step, res ipsa loquitur/unequivocality, legal and factual impossibility, abandonment.

    (c) Assault: original definition, current status.

    (d) Solicitation: merger, abandonment, incomplete communication.

    (e) Conspiracy: inference, merger, Pinkerton liability, overt act, vicarious liability (MPC), prosecutors' love, multiple crimes, wheel vs. chain, withdrawal, inferring intent, Wharton's Rule, legislative exemption defense.

7. Accomplice liability.

    (a) Derivative liability, conduct, common law categories vs. modern status, justification vs. excuse, legislative exemption defense, abandonment, innocent agency doctrine.

§ 2 Basic Principles of Criminal Law

2.1 Introduction

1. Henry Hart argues that criminal law is a method with five features:

   (a) It operates by a series of commands ("don't kill or steal").

   (b) A community makes the commands binding.

   (c) There are sanctions for disobeying the commands.

   (d) The distinction between civil and criminal sanctions is that criminal violations draw a community's moral condemnation.

   (e) Violations are punished.

2. Murray: laws are framed as conditions ("if you do x, then y"—e.g., punishment), emphasizing **agency and choice.**

3. **The legality principle**: *Nullem crimen sine lege, nulla poene sine lege* ("no crime without law, no punishment without law").

4. Sources of criminal law:

   (a) Codification (statutes, administrative rules, etc.).

   (b) Common law (based on the English system, as distinct from a civil-law system).

   (c) Case law.

   (d) Model Penal Code.

5. Themes in criminal law;

   (a) What is a crime? What is criminal law for?

   (b) What distinguishes criminal conduct?

   (c) Why do we use criminal law to address wrongs rather than another system (torts, contracts)?

   (d) How do we punish crime? What are the limits on punishment?

6. What distinguishes criminal punishment?

   (a) Criminal penalties can restrain personal liberty (but civil penalties don't).

   (b) Moral stigma.

   (c) Judgment is collective—it isn't about two parties.[1]

7. **Probable cause** is necessary to make an arrest.

---

[1] See Schelling, "Ethics, Law, and the Exercise of Self-Command."

8. **Indictment** by a grand jury is usually necessary before a case can go to trial.

9. The Sixth Amendment guarantees a right to a speedy and public trial by an impartial jury.

10. **Due process clauses** in the Fifth and Fourteenth amendments guarantee persuasion **beyond a reasonable doubt** (as determined by the factfinder—either a judge or jury).

11. The Tenth Amendment reserves unenumerated powers for the states.

2.1.1 Beyond a Reasonable Doubt: *Owens v. State*

Circumstantial evidence can meet the reasonable doubt standard. The definition of "beyond a reasonable doubt" is contested and jury instructions vary.

1. Owens was found drunk and asleep behind the wheel of a running car in a private driveway.

2. Circumstantial evidence gave equal weight to two interpretations of the facts: either he had just arrived (which would make him guilty of driving while intoxicated) or had not yet left (not guilty).

3. If each interpretation is equally likely, the factfinder could not fairly choose the guilty option beyond a reasonable doubt. But after analyzing the evidence, the court found "the totality of the circumstances are, in the last analysis, inconsistent with a reasonable hypothesis of innocence."[2]

4. The trial court convicted him of driving while intoxicated. The appellate court affirmed.

2.2 Principles of Punishment

1. Some types of punishment: prison, fines, community service, shaming.

2. Two key questions:

    (a) Who should be punished?

    (b) How much punishment is appropriate?

3. There are two predominant (and non-mutually-exclusive) theories of punishment: **retributivism** and **utilitarianism**.

---

[2]Casebook p. 17.

2.2.1 Utilitarianism

Punishment is justified because it's useful.

1. Jeremy Bentham: the **principle of utility** evaluates actions in light of their effect on the happiness of the interested party. Laws aim to augment a community's total happiness.

2. Kent Greenawalt: "Since punishment involves pain, it can be justified only if it accomplishes enough good consequences to outweigh this harm."[3] The consequences of an action determine its morality (or, the ends justify the means).

3. Goals of utilitarian punishment:

    (a) General deterrence (i.e., discourage an action from occurring in general within a community).

    (b) Specific deterrence (i.e., discourage a specific person from doing something harmful).

    (c) Incapacitation.

    (d) Reform.

2.2.2 Retributivism

Punishment is justified because criminals deserve it.

1. Michael Moore: "the desert of an offender is a sufficient reason to punish him or her."[4]

2. Immanuel Kant: penal law is a categorical imperative.

3. James Fitzjames Stephen: **assaultive retribution** holds that hatred and vengeance in the name of morality are socially beneficial. Punishment expresses our collective hatred. Criminals are "noxious insects."[5]

4. Herbert Morris: **protective retribution** holds that rules exist to provide collective benefit. They guards against unfair advantage for freeriders. If somebody cheats, punishment evens the score.

5. Jeffrey G. Murphy & Jean Hampton: **victim vindication retribution** wrongdoers implicitly place their own value above their victims'; "retributive punishment is the defeat of the wrongdoer at the hands of the victim."[6]

---

[3]Casebook p. 35.
[4]Casebook p. 39.
[5]Casebook p. 42.
[6]Casebook p. 46.

2.2.3 Justifying Punishment

2.2.3.1 Retributive and Utilitarian Justifications for Punishment: *The Queen v. Dudley and Stephens*

Utilitarian and retributivist justifications for punishment can lead to divergent results.

1. Dudley, Stephens, Brooks, and Parker were castaways on a boat 1600 miles from the Cape of Good Hope. They quickly ran out of food and water. After twenty days, Dudley and Stephens decided to kill and eat Parker (with Brooks dissenting). All of them ate Parker's body for four days, at which point they were rescued and brought to trial.

2. The court found them guilty of murder. They were pardoned soon after.

3. This case highlights the differences between retributive and utilitarian theories of justice. Parker was weak and unlikely to have survived the last four days before rescue arrived. Dudley and Stephens likely wouldn't have survived, either. Moreover, Dudley and Stephens had family responsibilities, while Parker was a drifter.

4. A retributive response would find that Dudley and Stephens are morally culpable and should be found guilty regardless of the mitigating factors.

5. A utilitarian response would find them not guilty on the recognition of a net benefit for all parties involved (except Parker, but he would have died regardless). However, a utilitarian might want to deter castaways from eating each other in case they end up being rescued.

2.2.3.2 Sentencing: *People v. Du*

Courts can draw on both utilitarian and retributivist rationals in sentencing.

1. The defendant, Soon Ja Du, a 51-year-old woman, owned a liquor store in LA. A 15-year-old girl, Latasha Harlins, in the store put a bottle of orange juice in her backpack. It's not clear whether she intended to pay. A fight ensued, in which Du was injured. As Harlins was leaving, Du pulled out a gun (which had been previously stolen, modified to fire on a hair trigger, and then recovered) and shot Harlins in the back of the head.

2. Du testified that she did not intend to kill Harlins. The jury rejected her defense and convicted her of voluntary manslaughter.

3. Du's probation officer concluded she "would be most unlikely to repeat this or any other crime." The sentencing court sentenced Du to ten years, but suspended the sentence and placed her on probation. The probation officer wrote, "it is my opinion that justice is never served when public opinion, prejudice, revenge or unwarranted sympathy are considered by a

sentencing court in resolving a case." She tested Du's case against seven goals of sentencing:

   (a) Protect society.
   (b) Punish the defendant.
   (c) Encourage the defendant to lead a law-abiding life.
   (d) Deter others.
   (e) Incapacitation.
   (f) Secure restitution for the victim.
   (g) Seek uniformity in sentencing.

4. None of these reasons were sufficient to justify prison time. The only somewhat convincing motivation for prison time was the strong presumption against probation when guns are involved. But this was an unusual case, she concluded, "which overcomes the statutory presumption against probation."

2.3 Proportionality of Punishment

2.3.1 General Principles

1. Kant: The "right of retaliation" (*jus talionis*) is "the only principle which in regulating a public court...can definitely assign both the quality and the quantity of a just penalty."[7] Murderers must be punished with death.

2. Bentham: punishment has four goals:

   (a) General deterrence.
   (b) Encourage criminals to choose the lesser of two offenses.
   (c) Encourage criminals to do no more mischief than necessary.
   (d) Punish cheaply.

3. ...and five rules:

   (a) To effectively deter, the value of the punishment must be greater than the value of the offense.
   (b) The greater the mischief, the greater the punishment.
   (c) Punishment must be sufficient to induce criminals to choose the lesser of two crimes.
   (d) Punishment must be adapted to each offense.
   (e) Punishment should not be greater than necessary.

4. The *Eighth Amendment* prohibits disproportionate and cruel and unusual punishment. MPC § 1.02(2)(c) is in accord.

---

[7]Casebook p. 70.

2.3.2 Constitutional Principles

2.3.2.1 Rape and Capital Punishment: *Coker v. Georgia*

Rape does not involve the taking of life. The death penalty is therefore a disproportionate punishment in violation of the Eighth Amendment.

1. The defendant escaped from prison, where he was serving time for multiple violent felonies. He broke into the Carvers' house, tied up Mr. Carver, and kidnapped and raped Mrs. Carver.

2. The Supreme Court held that the Georgia jury's death sentence violated the Eight Amendment, because rape is a crime "not involving the taking of life." In their dissent, Justices Burger and Rehnquist argued that the Eight Amendment does not prohibit states from taking prior behavior into account. While the death penalty may be disproportionate to the current crime, it can act as an effective deterrent.

3. A related case, *Kennedy v. Louisiana*, involved the rape of a child. The court narrowly upheld that the death penalty was "grossly disproportionate" for rape, but Justice Alito issued a scathing dissent questioning the argument that every murder is more "morally depraved" than every rape.

2.3.2.2 Three Strikes: *Ewing v. California*

Recidivism can justify harsh punishments.

1. Ewing stole three golf clubs from a pro shop. With multiple prior felony convictions, California's three strikes law required a minimum sentence of 25 years, which Ewing argued violated the Eighth Amendment.

2. Justice O'Connor:

    (a) In *Harmelin v. Michigan*, Justice Kennedy laid out a set of principles for determining proportionality:

    i. The primacy of the legislature.
    ii. The variety of legitimate penological schemes.
    iii. Federalism.
    iv. Objectivity.
    v. **The Eighth Amendment does not require strict proportionality. It only forbids "grossly disproportionate" sentences.**

    (b) The court upheld Ewing's 25-year sentence, arguing that "Ewing's sentence is justified by the State's public-safety interest in incapacitating and deterring recidivist felons..."[8]

---
[8]Casebook p. 85.

3. Justice Scalia concurring: the justification for the sentence has nothing to do with proportionality and everything to do with the idea that "punishment should reasonably pursue the multiple purposes of the criminal law" (incapacitation, deterrence, retribution, rehabilitation).

4. Justice Breyer, dissenting: compared two prior cases, *Rummel* and *Solem*, which both involved major prison sentences for recidivist felons who committed relatively small crimes. In *Solem*, the court found the sentence to be too long, and upheld the sentence in *Rummel*. *Ewing* falls in the "twilight zone" between the two. Given that ambiguity, 25 years to life is grossly disproportionate to the crime of shoplifting golf clubs.

2.4 Statutory Interpretation

2.4.1 The Legality Principle

1. *Nullem crimen sine lege, nulla poene sine lege*: "no crime without law, no punishment without law." A person cannot be convicted and punished unless her conduct was defined as criminal.

2. Three corollaries:

    (a) Statutes should be understandable to ordinary people.

    (b) Statutes should not delegate policy matters on an ad hoc basis.

    (c) **Lenity doctrine**: ambiguous statutes should be interpreted in favor of the accused.

3. Rationales:

    (a) Prevents arbitrary and vindictive application of law.

    (b) Enhances individual autonomy by allowing people to act without fear of retroactive punishment.

    (c) Provides fair warning so that people can conform their behavior to the law.

4. Constitutional foundations:

    (a) *Ex post facto* clause.[9]

    (b) Bill of attainder clause.[10]

    (c) Fifth Amendment.

    (d) Fourteenth Amendment.

5. **Institutional competency**: courts should not preempt the legislature's role.

---
[9] Art. I, §9, cl. 3.
[10] Art. I, § 9, cl. 3.

2 BASIC PRINCIPLES OF CRIMINAL LAW

6. **Principle of statutory clarity**: a criminal statute must not be "so vague that men of common intelligence must necessarily guess at its meaning and differ as to its application."[11] Rationales: same as for the lenity doctrine. Constitutional foundations: Fifth and Fourteenth Amendments.

2.4.2 Crime without Law: *Commonwealth v. Mochan*

For a defendant to be convicted and punished, he must have violated a defined law. Catch-all offenses like "injuriously affecting public morality" can suffice.

1. The defendant repeatedly made lewd phone calls to a married woman.

2. His conduct was not prohibited by statute, and no precedential case dealt with the same question.

3. The trial judge found the defendant guilty of "intending to debauch and corrupt, and further devising and intending to harass, embarrass, and vilify."[12].

4. The appellate court held that solicitation of adultery on its own is not indictable, but it affirmed the conviction on the grounds that the defendant's acts "injuriously affected public morality."

5. The dissent raised an **institutional competency** issue, arguing that the courts should not preempt the legislature's role in defining new crimes.

2.4.3 Statutory Interpretation and Institutional Competence: *Keeler v. Superior Court*

Institutional competence prevents courts from rewriting statutes in interpreting them. If a statute's meaning is ambiguous, the court must look to legislative intent and common law meanings.

1. A man punched his pregnant ex-wife in the stomach, causing the death of her fetus. He was charged with murder.

2. The question before the California Supreme Court was whether an unborn fetus was a "human being" under the California statutory definition of murder. The court examined common law definitions of murder and concluded that it was intended to protect people who had been "born alive" but that it did not protect unborn fetuses.

3. The prosecution argued that medical advances had shifted the definition of a "viable" fetus such that an unborn fetus could be considered a "human being." The court held, however, that such a ruling "would indeed be to rewrite the statute under the guise of construing it."[13]

---

[11] *Connally v. Gen. Constr. Co.*, 269 U.S. 385, 391 (1926).
[12] Casebook p. 92–93
[13] Casebook p. 99.

4. The dissent argued a different interpretation of common law in which a "quickened" fetus could be considered a human being.

5. Soon after this case, the state legislature amended the California murder statute to apply to fetuses.

2.4.4 Statutory Clarity: *In re Banks*

Statutes can be found unconstitutional if they are so indefinite as to fail to give fair notice and fail to "define a reasonably ascertainable standard of guilt."

1. The defendant was charged under a peeping tom statute that prohibited "secretly peeping into room occupied by female person."

2. The defendant argued the statute was unconstitutional because, if read literally, it would outlaw a wide range of obviously lawful conduct (e.g., looking through a keyhole in your child's bedroom door to make sure she had fallen asleep).

3. The court reasoned that statutes can be found unconstitutional if they are so indefinite as to fail to give fair notice and fail to "define a reasonably ascertainable standard of guilt."[14] In this case, however, the meaning of "secretly" is well enough defined to describe invasion of privacy.

2.4.5 Void for Vagueness: *City of Chicago v. Morales*

Statutes that fail to clearly define criminal conduct and delineate it from lawful conduct are void for vagueness.

1. The Chicago city council enacted an ordinance prohibiting "criminal street gang members" from "loitering."

2. Justice Stevens: "...the vagueness that dooms this ordinance is not the product of uncertainty about the normal meaning of 'loitering,' but rather about what loitering is covered by the ordinance and what is not."[15] Under the new statute, ordinary people "might unwittingly engage in forbidden loitering," and law enforcement has too much discretion.

3. Justice O'Connor, concurring, suggested specific language the legislature might have adopted.

4. Justice Scalia, dissenting: legislatures are free to regulate against harmless conduct, and in doing so they do not violate the constitution.

---

[14] Casebook p. 105.
[15] Casebook p. 115.

2.4.6 Interpreting Statutory Language: *Muscarello v. United States*

A statute's meaning can turn on a single word. Courts are charged with interpreting statutory language.

1. The question was whether the term "carry" in a firearm statute included carrying in a car, or whether it was restricted to carrying on the person.

2. Justice Breyer traced the definition of the word in a range of contexts, including a brief empirical reading of news stories, to argue that it includes carrying in a car.

3. Justice Ginsburg dissented with her own range of examples pointing in the opposite direction, and argued that the lenity principle should resolve the ambiguity in favor of the defendant.

§ 3 Elements of a Crime

1. Every crime has two elements: **actus reus** and **mens rea**.

2. Every crime also has attendant circumstances.

3.1 Actus Reus

1. Literally, "guilty act." There is no universally accepted definition. In murder, for instance, some would consider it to be the pulling of the trigger. Others would consider it to be the death itself. The most common definition would consider it to be both.

2. Under both common law and the MPC, voluntary acts are the products of free will. We do not not punish acts that are not the product of the individual's free will.

3. "Omissions are not accidents."—Marianne Moore.

4. What constitutes an act? When does the act begin? See Model Penal Code § 2.01.

5. If someone holds a gun to your head and tells you to act, your act is voluntary. **An act is something you do willfully.**

6. Thought crimes are not punishable (*Minority Report*, *Firestarter*).

7. The **harm principle**: we punish acts that are socially and individually harmful. However, there are constitutional limits on what the state can criminalize. The state may not criminalize behavior it believes to be immoral or distasteful unless it causes actual harm. See *Lawrence* below.

8. **Laws can only punish *conduct*, not status.** For instance, a city cannot make it a crime to be addicted to a substance.

9. **Omissions and duty**: Criminal liability for omissions exists only where there is a legal duty to act. Criminal law is reluctant to create positive responsibilities, but **there are a few common law relationships where such responsibilities exist**: e.g., parent-child, spouse-spouse, master-servant. Other circumstances giving rise to legal duty include contracts, statutes, voluntarily assuming care and prevent others from assisting, and creating harm to another. See *Beardsley* below.

10. Under the MPC, omissions do not create criminal liability unless (1) the law expressly makes the omission sufficient or (2) the duty is otherwise imposed by law.[16]

---
[16] MPC § 2.01(3).

3 ELEMENTS OF A CRIME

3.1.1 Voluntary vs. Involuntary Action: *Martin v. State*

We do not punish involuntary actions.

1. Police officers took a drunk man from his home and onto a public highway, where they then arrested him for public drunkenness. The court held that public drunkenness cannot be established when the accused was involuntarily carried to a public place.

3.1.2 Proving Involuntary Action: *State v. Utter*

"Act" is synonymous with "voluntary act." An involuntary or unconscious act cannot establish guilt.

1. Defendant was drunk and stabbed his son. He had no memory of the stabbing. He argued that his service in the army had caused him to develop a "conditioned response" which makes him react violently and involuntarily to people approaching unexpectedly from behind.

2. The court reasoned that an "act" requires voluntary action—that is, "act" is synonymous with "voluntary act." An involuntary or unconscious act cannot induce guilt—that is, it is not an "act" at all.

3. The court found that the defendant's theory of conditioned response should have been presented to a jury *if there was substantial evidence to support it*. However, because the jury could not possibly know or infer what had happened in the room at the time of the stabbing, the question should not be sent to the jury.

3.1.3 Legal Duty to Act: *People v. Beardsley*

Criminal law is reluctant to create positive responsibilities, but there are a few common law relationships where such responsibilities exist: e.g., parent-child, spouse-spouse, master-servant. (See the beginning of this section under "Actus Reus" for other circumstances, e.g. contracts, giving rise to legal duty.)

1. While his wife was away, the defendant was drinking heavily at his house with another woman. The woman took several tablets of morphine and became unresponsive. The defendant put her in a basement room in his house (which another man was renting). The woman died that evening.

2. The issue was whether the defendant had a legal duty to protect the woman. If he had omitted to perform his duty, he would have been criminally liable for manslaughter.

3. The prosecution argued that the defendant was in the role of the woman's guardian.

3 ELEMENTS OF A CRIME

4. The court reasoned that if the defendant had been drinking with a man and that man attempted suicide, the defendant would not have had a duty to protect him—so it should make no difference that he was with a woman.

5. The lower courts convicted the defendant of manslaughter, but the Michigan Supreme Court here reversed.

3.1.4 Failure to Act: *Barber v. Superior Court*

Omissions do not establish culpability absent a legal duty to act.

1. A patient suffered cardiac arrest after surgery. Doctors managed to save him, but he suffered significant brain damage. He remained in a vegetative state on life support with little chance of recovery. His family decided to remove him from life support, and he died a few days later

2. The question before the court was whether his doctors had a duty to keep him alive—since omitting to perform that duty would make them liable for murder. **"There is no criminal liability for failure to act unless there is a legal duty to act."**

3. The court reasoned that removing the man from life support constituted an omission, not a positive act. The decision of whether to continue treatment was left to the family. Therefore, the doctors did not unlawfully fail to perform a legal duty.

3.1.5 Constitutional Limitations on Criminalizing Conduct: *Lawrence v. Texas*

There are constitutional limits on the behavior states can criminalize.

1. The issue was whether a Texas law criminalizing sodomy violated the Fourteenth Amendment's Due Process Clause and equal protection guarantee.

2. Justice Kennedy:

    (a) The statute violated individuals' rights to privacy and liberty.

    (b) The Supreme Court had previously ruled on a similar Georgia statute outlawing sodomy in *Bowers v. Hardwick*: "*Bowers* was not correct when it was decided, and it is not correct today. It ought not to remain binding precedent."

    (c) The equal protection guarantee ensures that homosexuals are entitled to the same privacy protections as heterosexuals.

    (d) The Constitution limits states' power to outlaw social harms.

3.2 Mens Rea

3.2.1 General Principles

1. "Guilty mind."

2. *Actus non facit reum nisi mens sit rea*: the act does not make a person guilty unless the mind be also guilty.

3. *United States v. Cordoba-Hincapie*: a brief history of the evolution from ancient English strict liability to the modern requirement of a guilty state of mind.[17]

4. Under the MPC, mental states (purposely, etc.) **apply distributively to all elements of the crime and attendant circumstances**. Common law jurisdictions vary. E.g., if the statute bans "knowingly shooting a deer in Alameda County," the MPC requires knowledge of (1) shooting a deer and (2) being in Alameda County.

5. There are two usages of mens rea:

    (a) **Culpability**: a morally culpable state of mind in general.

    (b) **Elemental**: the mental state specified in the definition of the crime.

6. The general "culpability" variant has given way to the "elemental" variant. See *Cunningham* below.

7. The MPC follows the elemental variant, i.e., the actor must have the specific state of mind required in the definition of the crime. See notes on § 2.02 below.

8. Under **transferred intent**, we attribute liability to a defendant who, intending to act against one person, accidentally acts against another person instead. See *Conley* below.

9. **Specific and general intent**: see below.

10. **Willful blindness**: see below, "Knowledge of Attendant Circumstances and Willful Blindness."

3.2.1.1 General Culpability: *Regina v. Cunningham* Maliciousness requires intent or recklessness, not a generally culpable state of mind.

1. The defendant stole a coin-operated gas meter from the basement of his mother-in-law's house, causing noxious gas to escape and partially asphyxiate his neighbor.

---

[17]Casebook p. 149.

3 ELEMENTS OF A CRIME

2. The issue was whether his action was malicious. A lower court convicted the defendant on the definition of malice as "wickedness," i.e., a generally culpable state of mind.

3. The appellate court defined malice as (1) an **intention** to do the specific harm, or (2) **recklessness** (i.e., he foresaw that the harm might occur, but did it anyway). In this case, there was no malice directed at Mrs. Wade. The court overturned the conviction.

3.2.1.2 Transferred Intent: *People v. Conley*

1. In a fight after a high school party, the defendant smashed a wine bottle into the victim's face, causing permanent disability. He intended to hit someone else (who ducked), but the court found that the defendant's words and demeanor nonetheless intended his action to cause permanent disability.

2. The common law definition of intent includes both the actor's conscious goal and the results that are "virtually certain to occur"[18]—similar to substantial certainty in intentional torts.

3. A person "intends the natural and probable consequences of his actions." The Fourteenth Amendment prevents courts from presuming this, but juries can use common sense to recognize it.

4. **Transferred intent** allows transfer from one victim to another. Transfer between different types of harms is less clear cut. Courts often apply it, but not always.

3.2.1.3 Specific and General Intent

1. There is dispute about the meaning of "general intent" and "specific intent." The most common version (and Murray's preferred version):[19]

    (a) **General**: the actor only desired to commit the criminal offense conduct–e.g., rape (unlawful carnal knowledge of a woman), battery (harmful or offensive contact).

---

[18]Casebook p. 155.

[19]Other versions of the specific/general intent distinction:

(a) General: the definition of the crime sets out no specific mental state, so the prosecutor needs only to prove a generally culpable state of mind. Specific: the definition of a crime explicitly sets out a mental state.

(b) General: reserved for crimes that permit conviction on the basis of a less culpable mental state (e.g., negligence or recklessness). Specific: denotes an offense that includes a definition of intent or knowledge.

(b) **Specific**: the actor acted with an additional "special mental element"—e.g., murder (intentional killing *with malice aforethought*), larceny (taking away the property of another *with the intent to deprive him of it permanently*). Subcategories:

   i. Intent to commit a future act—e.g., possession *with intent to distribute*.

   ii. Special motive—e.g., offensive contact *intended to cause humiliation* or intentional killing *with malice aforethought*.

   iii. Knowledge of attendant circumstances—e.g., sale of obscene material *to a minor*.

2. Most jurisdictions and the MPC have abandoned the distinction between general and specific intent crimes. It most often comes up in cases inolving intoxication and mistake of fact.

3.2.1.4 Common Law Specific Intent Crimes: BAFFLEPACK

1. At common law, there are ten specific intent crimes (BAFFLEPACK):

   (a) Burglary.

   (b) Assault.

   (c) False pretenses.

   (d) Forgery.

   (e) Larceny.

   (f) Embezzlement.

   (g) Premeditated murder.

   (h) Attempt.

   (i) Conspiracy/solicitation.

   (j) Kidnapping for ransom.

3.2.1.5 MPC § 2.02: General Requirements of Culpability

1. **The MPC requires "elemental" culpability**—i.e., the specific state of mind required in the definition of the crime, rather than a generally morally culpable state of mind.

2. The MPC abandons the elemental-culpable distinction. Most jurisdictions have adopted the MPC's approach in whole or in part.

3. There are four levels of culpability in the MPC:[20]

   (a) **Purpose**: An actor intends to perform a specific action or to cause a specific result.

---
[20]MPC § 2.02(2).

(b) **Knowledge**: An actor is aware of factual circumstances that establish criminal culpability, and if the element involves a result of his conduct, he is practically certain that the result will occur.

(c) **Recklessness**: An actor creates and recognizes a substantial, unjustifiable risk and acts anyway. The jury should decide whether the risk is substantial and unjustifiable and whether *disregard of the risk* deserves condemnation.

(d) **Negligence**: An actor inadvertently creates a substantial, unjustifiable risk of which he should have been aware. The jury should decide whether the risk is substantial and unjustifiable and whether the defendant's *failure to perceive the risk* deserves condemnation.

4. If a law does not specify a culpable state of mind (i.e., no mens rea), culpability is established if the person acted purposefully, knowingly, or recklessly. **Negligence is excluded unless the law specifically prescribes it** (although many jurisdictions do not exclude negligence). This tracks the common law approach. According to the ALI commentary, "since negligence is an exceptional basis of liability, it should be excluded as a basis unless explicitly prescribed."[21]

3.2.1.6 Knowledge of Attendant Circumstances and Willful Blindness

1. **Willful blindness** means suspecting the truth but not investigating it.

2. MPC § 2.02(7): where "knowledge of the existence of a particular fact is an element of the offense, such knowledge is established if a person is aware of a high probability of its existence."

3.2.1.7 Defining Knowledge: *State v. Nations*

Mens rea requirements depend on statutory language.

1. The defendant, Sandra Nations, operated a bar where a sixteen-year-old girl was dancing for money.

2. A Missouri child welfare statute imposed criminal liability on anyone who knowingly aided such activity.

3. The Model Penal Code in § 2.02(7) holds that "knowledge" of a particular element of a crime is established when the actor is aware of a "high probability of its existence"—i.e., willful blindness towards a fact constitutes knowledge of that fact.

4. The Missouri statute, however, did not adopt this definition of "knowledge." The court thus found the defendant to be reckless, but not knowing, and held in favor of the defendant.

---

[21]MPC § 2.02(3). See also ALI commentary, casebook pp. 159–63, and for commentary on § 2.02(3) specifically, p. 162 n. 5.

3.2.2 Strict Liability

1. Strict liability crimes assign guilt without requiring mens rea.

2. **Public-welfare offenses** are strict liability. See *Cordoba-Hincapie* below.

3. If a statute is silent on the mens rea, courts can look to common law definitions. See *Staples* and *Garnett* below.

4. Strict liability offenses are usually *malum prohibitum* public welfare offenses with light penalties. Statutory rape is the major exception.

3.2.2.1 Public Welfare Offenses: *United States v. Cordoba-Hincapie*

1. One category of strict liability crimes are "public-welfare offenses"—e.g., liquor laws, anti-narcotics laws, motor vehicle regulations.

2. Public-welfare laws are meant to regulate administrative offenses unrelated to questions of personal guilt.

3. mens rea is probably required if the punishment of the wrongdoer far outweighs regulation of the social order.

4. mens rea is probably not required if the punishment is light (e.g., small fine and no prison time).

5. Even when a statute is silent on the mens rea requirement, it can still sometimes be interpreted as requiring a minimal level of mens rea. See *Staples* below.

6. With strict liability offenses, there is no basis for acquittal on the grounds of mistakes of fact or law. **It doesn't matter what you intended to do—it only matters that you did it.**

3.2.2.2 Inferring Mens Rea: *Staples v. United States*

If a statute is silent on the mens rea, courts can look to the common law for guidance. Strict liability generally should only be imposed for public welfare offenses. The severity of the punishment can also impact the analysis.

Also, the defendant must know every fact that gave rise to his legal obligation.

1. BATF agents found the defendant in possession of an unregistered semi-automatic AR-15 rifle that had been modified to shoot as an automatic weapon. Under the National Firearms Act, this gun was classified as a machine gun and was required to be registered.

2. The defendant argued that he didn't know the gun had been modified, and therefore he should be shielded from criminal liability for failing to register it. The District Court and the Court of Appeals rejected his argument.

3. Justice Thomas:

    (a) The relevant statute is silent concerning the mens rea requirement.

    (b) Common law holds that a mens rea should be required here, despite the statute's silence, unless it's clear that Congress intended to remove the mens rea requirement.

    (c) The prosecution argued that Congress intended this statute to address "public welfare" offense, and thus impose strict criminal liability.

    (d) This interpretation of Congress's silence (says Thomas) has typically been applied to situations where the regulated offense poses a very clear threat to public safety (e.g., hand grenades in *Freed* or narcotics in *Balint*). In contrast, possession of items with no public safety threat has not been held to be a strict liability crime (e.g., food stamps in *Liparota*).

    (e) Gun ownership is generally an innocent activity (half of American households own a gun), unlike possessing a hand grenade or selling hard drugs.

    (f) The severe penalty here (10 years) negates the public welfare rationale. Generally, mens rea should be required as part of statutes defining felony offenses.

    (g) If Congress wanted to impose severe criminal penalties on gun owners who unknowingly possessed certain offending weapons (like machine guns), it would have said so explicitly.

4. Justice Stevens, dissenting:

    (a) This statute is not based on a common law crime. We cannot rely on common law to fill Congress's omissions. Rather, we should assume Congress's omissions are intentional.

    (b) Machine guns are "dangerous [and] deleterious devices." This is clearly a public welfare statute.

3.2.2.3 Legislative Silence as Strict Liability: *Garnett v. State*

Legislative context can indicate that the omission of a mens rea is deliberate, i.e., that the legislature intended to define a strict liability crime.

1. The adult defendant had sex with someone he did not know was below the age of consent. The statutory rape language did not specify a mens rea component. The trial court convicted him of statutory rape.

2. The appellate court noted that in statutes that do not define a mens rea component, the **MPC generally recognizes strict liability only for offenses that do not give rise to any "legal disability."**[22]

---
[22] Casebook p. 189.

3 ELEMENTS OF A CRIME

3. In this case, however, the court pointed out that the legislature was explicit about mens rea in the previous section, so its silence in the section at hand was likely deliberate. Therefore, it likely intended statutory rape to be a strict liability crime. The court upheld the conviction.

4. The dissent argued that the legislative history and structure suggest that there is a mens rea component.

3.2.3 Mistake and Mens Rea

1. **Good faith mistakes do not have to be reasonable to be valid defenses against crimes with mens rea components.**

2. Why limit the application of the mistake doctrine?

    (a) Utilitarianism: we want people to know the law.

    (b) Retributivism: hard to say; retributivists might actually want a broad application of the mistake doctrine, since unwitting offenders may not be morally culpable.

3. *Malum in se*: bad in itself—e.g., murder.

4. *Malum prohibitum*: bad because outlawed—e.g., driving without a license.

3.2.3.1 Common Law vs. MPC Mistake of Law and Fact

Common law mistake of fact:	MPC mistake of fact:
1. Specific intent crimes (i.e., BAFFLEPACK): mistake of fact, whether reasonable or not, will negate the mens rea for a crime. 2. General intent crimes (e.g., rape): mistake of fact will *not* negate the mens rea unless the mistake was reasonable.	1. Mistake of fact is a defense when it "negatives" a "material element of the offense."[23] 2. The MPC does not distinguish between specific and general intent crimes. 3. Recall § 2.02(3): "When the culpability sufficient to establish a material element of an offense is not prescribed by law, such element is established if a person acts purposely, knowingly or recklessly with respect thereto." Negligence is excluded.
Common law mistake of law: *ignorantia legis neminem excusat* ("ignorance of the law is no excuse"), with a few exceptions (which are the same as the MPC mistake of law elements below).	**MPC mistake of law** defense is available when: 1. There is a lack of fair notice.[24] This exception is typically reserved for *malum prohibitum* crimes that criminalize passive behavior. 2. The actor reasonably relied on an official statement of the law. See *Marerro* below. 3. The ignorance negatives a mental element of the offense (e.g., in *Cheek* below, if the defendant was unaware of the duty to file and pay taxes, he could not be found guilty of *willful* tax evasion.)

3.2.3.2 Mistake of Fact: *People v. Navarro* For specific intent crimes, it doesn't matter whether a mistake of fact is reasonable.

1. The defendant stole four wooden beams from a construction site. He believed in good faith that the owner had abandoned the beams.

2. The trial court instructed the jury that the defendant would not guilty of theft if he *reasonably* believed in good faith that the beams had been abandoned or that he had permission to take them. The jury found the defendant guilty of theft.

3. The appellate court reversed, reasoning that if the defendant believed in good faith that he was allowed to take the beams—regardless of whether that belief was reasonable—he lacked the intent necessary for theft. (A jury could infer that a defendant does not hold such a belief in good faith—but in this case, his belief was genuine.)

3.2.3.3 Mistake of Law: *People v. Marrero* Misreading a statute does not entitle a defendant to a mistake of law defense. However, reasonable reliance on an official source can make the defense available.

1. A federal prison guard was charged with possessing an unlicensed loaded pistol at a club. He argued that he interpreted a state statute as exempting "peace officers" from the gun law—but in fact, the statute only exempted state penal corrections officers, not federal officers.

2. The trial court rejected the defendant's argument that his misunderstanding of the law exempted him from criminal liability. He relied on a New York statute that relieves criminal liability if the defendant mistakenly relies on "a statute or other enactment." The prosecution argued (and the court agreed) that misconstruing the meaning of a statute is not enough to establish a defense—drawing on MPC § 2.04(3), it argued the statute must actually be "determined to be invalid or erroneous." The appellate court reasoned that allowing defendants to simply interpret the law case-by-case would lead to chaos.

3. The dissent argued that there is no retributivist or utilitarian justification for punishing the defendant in this case. It argued further that the defendant reasonably interpreted the statute exempting "peace officers" and that he had no way of knowing that the courts would later interpret the statute to exclude federal penal officers.

4. According to the dissent, the majority opinion ruled out *any* defense based on mistaken understandings of law. This is a misinterpretation of the reasons for the New York mistake-of-law statute—and the majority opinion's reliance on MPC 2.04(3) is puzzling since the New York legislature specifically rejected that part of the MPC. The dissent believed there should be room for "good-faith mistaken belief founded on a well-grounded interpretation" of official law.

3.2.3.4 Unreasonable Mistake of Law: *Cheek v. United States* For specific intent crimes, the defendant cannot be found guilty if he lacked the requisite intent because of a mistake of fact, even if that mistake was unreasonable.

1. The defendant stopped paying taxes in the early 1980s. He had been heavily involved in the anti-tax movement and genuinely believed that the income tax on wages is unconstitutional. Federal criminal tax offenses require specific intent to violate the law—they require *willful* failure to file and pay taxes (otherwise, we'd all be criminals for making mistakes on our tax returns). Cheek argues that he did not *willfully* fail to file or pay.

2. The lower courts rejected Cheek's argument against the validity of jury instructions requiring an "honest and reasonable" belief that he was not required to pay income tax (as did the lower courts in *Navarro*).

3. Justice White: the precise issue as whether the defendant was aware of his duty to pay taxes, "which cannot be true if the jury credits a good-faith misunderstanding and belief submission."[25] It does not matter if his belief was unreasonable (though, as in *Navarro*, the jury may infer that the belief was not in good faith). The Supreme Court reversed the Court of Appeals and held that Cheek could make his case to a jury.

4. Justice Blackmun, dissenting: this decision "will encourage taxpayers to cling to frivolous views of the law."

3.3 Causation

1. Causation is implicit in the concept of actus reus. It's the link between the prohibited act and the harmful result.

2. **Causation analysis has two steps**: (1) determine which acts were but-for causes and (2) determine which but-for causes were proximate causes. Several factors can break the causal chain—see below.

3. The MPC uses slightly different terminology than the common law, but the analysis is not meaningfully different.

4. **Cause-in-fact**: a person's actions caused the outcome in question.

5. **"But-for" test**: a defendant's conduct is a cause-in-fact of the outcome in question if the outcome would not have occurred *but for* the defendant's actions.

6. **"Substantial factor" test**: a minority of jurisdictions apply this test if two independent defendants commit two separate acts, each of which could have caused the prohibited result, neither act is a "but for" cause. This test determines whether the action was nonetheless a "substantial factor" in bringing about the prohibited result. This test is used only in a minority of jurisdictions.

---

[25] Casebook p. 212.

3 ELEMENTS OF A CRIME

(a) **The MPC does *not* use the substantial factor test.** In cases where separate acts resulted in the prohibited harm, the MPC subjects each act to the but-for test.

7. A but-for cause is a **proximate cause** when it has a close enough connection between the act and the resulting harm.

    (a) The MPC does *not* recognize proximate cause. Rather, the distance between the but-for cause and the resulting harm is a factor in evaluating the actor's culpability—e.g., if the connection is weak, the actor is likely not very culpable.

8. **Aggravation** is not a cause, but **acceleration** is. See *Oxendine* below.

9. Certain intervening acts can break the causal chain (these apply both to common law and MPC causation analysis; see *Velazquez* below):

    (a) *De minimis* **contribution** to social harm: where the defendant's action was an insubstantial contribution to the harmful result, in comparison to the intervening event, the defendant is relieved of liability.

    (b) **Intended consequences doctrine**: a voluntary act intended to bring about the harmful result will be considered a proximate cause of the harm, regardless of other intervening events.

    (c) **Omissions**: an omission will rarely, if ever, supersede defendant's earlier, operative wrongful act.

    (d) Foreseeability of the intervening cause:

    　　i. **Responsive (dependent) intervening causes**: defendant bears criminal responsibility for the harmful result to a victim who seeks to extricate himself or another from a dangerous situation created by defendant, even where the victim was contributorily negligent.

    　　ii. **Coincidental (independent) intervening causes**: an act that does not occur in response defendant's conduct may break the causal chain.

    (e) **Apparent-safety doctrine**: once the victim has reached a place of apparent safety, defendant's prior wrongful act is no longer causally operative.

    (f) **Voluntary human intervention**: the victim's deliberate, informed intervention may break the causal chain.

10. Causation issues typically arise in the context of homicide.

3.3.1 Actual Cause

3.3.1.1 Acceleration: *Oxendine v. State*   There is a distinction between accelerating and merely aggravating an injury.

1. The defendant's girlfriend pushed his six-year-old son into a bathtub, causing severe internal injury. Around 24 hours later, the defendant also hit his son repeatedly. His son died from his injuries soon after. Medical testimony was unable to isolate the mortal blow.

2. The trial court found both defendants guilty of manslaughter. The Supreme Court of Delaware, however, found that the prosecution proved that the defendant had not *accelerated* his son's death, but only aggravated it. The court found the defendant innocent of manslaughter but guilty of assault in the second degree.

3.3.2 Proximate Cause

1. The doctrine of proximate cause determines whether an event that satisfies the but-for standard should be held accountable for the resulting harm.

2. **Proximate cause answers the question of who is most culpable for the harm.**

3. **The MPC does not use the term "proximate cause."** Issues related to proximate cause are treated as relating to the actor's culpability. See MPC § 2.03(2)(b) and (3)(b).

3.3.2.1 Chain of Causation: *People v. Rideout*   Intervening causes that are not reasonably foreseeable break the chain of causation.

1. The defendant was driving drunk and hit a car. The car's driver and passenger suffered no major injuries, but the car was damaged enough so that the headlights no longer worked. After moving safely to the side of the road, the car's passenger entered the road to inspect the car to see if they could turn on the hazard lights, where he was struck and killed by an oncoming car. The trial court found the defendant guilty for the passenger's death. The question is whether the defendant's drunk driving was the proximate cause of the passenger's death.

2. The appellate court introduced the ideas of **intervening and superseding causes**. An intervening cause supersedes the original cause if the original actor could not reasonably foresee the second cause, i.e., if it breaks the chain of causation. Dressler divides the second cause into *responsive intervening causes*, which arise directly from the original cause, and *coincidental intervening causes*.

3. The appellate court also introduced the *apparent-safety doctrine*, which holds that the defendant's causation ceases when the victim has reached a place of apparent safety (e.g., far off on the side of the road).

4. The appellate court also introduced the idea of *voluntary human intervention*, which relieves the defendant's liability if the victim voluntarily enters into a dangerous situation (e.g., a road in the night without any lights).

5. The appellate court overruled the trial court, finding that the prosecution failed to establish proximate cause. It remanded the case for a new trial.

6. Later, the Michigan Supreme Court overturned the appellate court's assessment that a jury could not find proximate cause.

3.3.2.2 Superseding Intervening Cause: *Velazquez v. State* A victim's own act can constitute a superseding intervening cause.

1. The defendant and the victim were drag racing. After the race, the victim spun around his car, raced back to the starting line, and careened over a guardrail, dying instantly.

2. The trial court found that the defendant's participation in the drag race was a cause-in-fact of the victim's death. The appellate court found that the drag race had already ended when the victim decided to spin around and race back to the finish line—an act that superseded the defendant's cause-in-fact.

§ 4 Homicide

1. Homicide is a neutral term. It is not necessarily a crime.

4.1 Common Law vs. Model Penal Code

Common Law	Model Penal Code

1. Murder.
 	
(a) First-degree: premeditated/deliberated.
(b) Second-degree:
    i. Intent to kill without premeditation.[26]
    ii. "Depraved heart" killing/implied malice (unintentional–e.g., gross recklessness).
(c) Both degrees require malice aforethought:
    i. Intent to kill.
    ii. Intent to cause grievous bodily injury.
    iii. Depraved or abandoned heart.
    iv. Intent to commit a felony.
 	
2. Manslaughter.
 	
(a) Voluntary: requires provocation.
(b) Involuntary: includes negligence and recklessness (unintentional).
	1. Murder.
	
	(a) With purpose.
	(b) With knowledge.
	(c) With recklessness (unintentional). Recklessness is presumed if the actor is engaged in one of several enumerated felonies (this is the MPC's replacement of the felony-murder rule).
	
	2. Manslaughter.
	
	(a) With recklessness (unintentional).
	(b) Under extreme mental or emotional distress.
	
	3. Negligent homicide.

4.2 Intentional Killing

4.2.1 Murder

1. Premeditation is usually the distinction between first- and second-degree murder.

2. **The MPC does not distinguish between first- and second-degree murder.** Culpability is evaluated at sentencing.

3. There are four common law definitions of murder:[27]

    (a) Intent to kill.

    (b) Intent to cause grievous bodily harm.

    (c) "Depraved-heart murder" (i.e., extreme recklessness regarding homicidal risk).

    (d) Intent to commit a felony.

4. In 1794, Pennsylvania introduced the idea of degrees.

5. The MPC recognizes three kinds of criminal homicide: murder, manslaughter, and negligent homicide.

6. Premeditation/deliberation: **in cold blood.** See *Guthrie* (not enough time for premeditation to occur) and *Midgett/Forrest* (proving premeditation from circumstantial evidence) below.

7. Provocation: **in hot blood.** See *Girouard* (verbal ll provocation) below.

8. There are **four elements of the common law provocation defense**, all of which must be present:

    (a) The defendant acted in the heat of passion.

    (b) The passion was the result of provocation.

    (c) The defendant did not have a cooling off period.

    (d) There is a causal link between the provocation, the passion, and the homicide.

    (e) If a **reasonable person** would have been provoked under the circumstances, the **provocation mitigates murder to manslaughter.**

9. *The MPC does not recognize provocation* as a defense. It uses the **extreme mental or emotional distress (EMED)** standard.[28] Proving EMED is a very low threshold. A jury then determines whether a reasonable person would have been distressed under the circumstances as the person believed them to be. The factfinder may consider the defendant's situation but *not* the defendant's idiosyncratic moral values. See *Casassa* below.

10. The MPC **does not require a cooling off period for EMED.**

---
[27] Casebook p. 236.
[28] MPC § 210.3(1)(b).

4.2.1.1 Premeditation vs. Intent: *State v. Guthrie*

Premeditation is not the same as intent. Premeditation requires time to become fully conscious of what is intended. The minimum time necessary for premeditation is not exact, but courts have defined it as "long enough to afford a reasonable man time to subject the nature of his response to a 'second look.'"[29]

1. The defendant stabbed and killed a coworker after the coworker taunted him and snapped him in the nose with a towel.

2. The trial court found him guilty of first-degree murder. The defendant argued that the trial court's instructions to the jury were improper because "the terms wilful, deliberate, and premeditated were equated with a mere intent to kill."

3. The appellate court agreed with the defendant that "premeditation" cannot be synonymous with intent—rather, it must be long enough for the defendant to be "fully conscious of what he intended." Reversed.

4.2.1.2 Proving Premeditation: *Midgett v. State*

Circumstantial evidence can prove premeditation, but proving it can be difficult.

1. The defendant repeatedly abused his young son, who died from the injuries. The trial court found him guilty of first-degree murder, which required premeditation and deliberation.

2. The defendant argued that there was no premeditation, and the Supreme Court of Arkansas agreed.

3. The dissent argued that symptoms of malnourishment indicated starvation, but the majority argued that the evidence did not prove starvation.

4. Shortly after this case, the Arkansas legislature amended its criminal code to broaden first-degree murder to include "extreme indifference to the value of human life" of people fourteen years old or younger.

4.2.1.3 Circumstantial Evidence of Premeditation: *State v. Forrest*

Premeditation can be proved or disproved on the basis of several circumstantial factors, including:

1. Want of provocation on part of the deceased.

---

[29] *People v. Morrin.*

4 HOMICIDE

2. The defendant's conduct and statements (including threats) before, during, and after the killing.

3. Ill will between the parties.

4. Dealing of lethal blows after the victim has been rendered helpless.

5. Evidence of especially brutal killing.

6. Nature and number of the victim's wounds.

1. The defendant shot and killed his terminally ill father in the hospital. The trial court convicted him of first-degree murder.

2. The defendant argued that there was no premeditation or deliberation, and therefore no evidence to prove first-degree murder.

3. The appellate court upheld the conviction, noting that premeditation must be proved (or disproved) by circumstantial evidence, including provocation from the victim, the defendant's conduct and statements, ill will between the parties, lethal blows after the victim was rendered helpless, and evidence of an especially brutal killing.

4. In this case, the court found that the victim was laying helpless and did nothing to provoke the defendant, and that the defendant had earlier made statements about "putting his father out of his misery." It upheld the jury instructions regarding first-degree murder.

4.2.2 Manslaughter

1. **Provocation can mitigate murder to manslaughter.** Common law and the MPC diverge on what constitutes provocation.

2. **Five elements of common law provocation**, all of which must be present:[30]

    (a) There must have been adequate provocation.

    (b) The killing must have been in the heat of passion.

    (c) There must not have been a cooling off period.

    (d) There must have been a causal connection between the provocation, the passion, and the fatal act.

    (e) (The sorts of provocations that courts have allowed as defenses at common law are the sort of actions that have offended traditional notions of a man's honor—e.g., catching a wife in the act with another man.)

---
[30] Casebook p. 267.

3. **The MPC does not recognize provocation.** It replaces provocation with an **"emotional disturbance"** test.[31] Under the MPC, homicide constitutes manslaughter when:

    (a) The homicide is committed "under the influence of extreme mental or emotional disturbance."

    (b) There is a reasonable explanation or excuse for the mental or emotional disturbance under the circumstances as the defendant believed them to be. In other words, the excuse is reasonable if a reasonable person in the defendant's situation would have been disturbed.

    (c) (The cooling off period is not an issue under the MPC definition.)

4. For a gender critique of the MPC's rules of provocation, see Victoria Nourse, "Passion's Progress."

5. **Words are usually not enough to constitute provocation.** Words can be sufficient if they accompany a threat of intent and ability to cause bodily harm.[32] Some jurisdictions allow **"informative words"** (e.g, "your husband is having an affair with ...") to constitute provocation.

4.2.2.1 Verbal Provocation: *Girouard v. State*

Words do not constitute provocation without threat of bodily harm. Some jurisdictions, however, have recognized "informational" words as sufficient provocation (e.g., "your spouse is sleeping with X").

1. The defendant stabbed and killed his wife after she taunted him relentlessly. The trial court, in a bench trial, convicted him of second degree murder.

2. The defendant argued on appeal that the rule of provocation should be expanded to include verbal provocation. The appellate court relied on the rule that for provocation to mitigate a charge of murder, it must be "calculated to inflame the passion of a reasonable man and tend to cause him to act for the moment from passion to reason." The standard is objective.

3. The court found that words can constitute adequate provocation if they accompany intent and ability to cause bodily harm. That was not the case in this scenario, however. The court upheld the second-degree murder conviction.

---

[31] MPC 210.3(1)(b) at Casebook p. 1000.
[32] Casebook pp. 267–68.

4.2.2.2 Emotional Disturbance: *People v. Casassa*

Emotional disturbance is a defense only if a reasonable person would have been disturbed under the circumstances. Emotional disturbance is an objective standard.

1. The defendant stabbed and killed his neighbor out of jealousy. The trial court found him guilty of second-degree murder.

2. The defendant argued he was acting under "extreme emotional disturbance," which would reduce the charge to manslaughter.

3. The appellate court reasoned that the emotional disturbance must meet an objectively reasonable standard. In this case, the disturbance was a result of the defendant's unique mental state—i.e., a reasonable person would not have been so emotionally disturbed under the circumstances. Affirmed.

4.2.3 Unintentional Killing

1. **Implied malice** is required to prove murder from an unintentional killing.

2. At common law, implied malice requires a **"depraved heart"**—i.e., it involves acting with a conscious disregard for human life and conduct involving a high probability of death. See *Knoller* below.

3. **The MPC does not use the depraved heart standard.** Under the MPC, ordinary recklessness proves manslaughter. It proves murder when the actor's "conscious disregard for the risk, under the circumstances, manifests extreme indifference to the value of human life"[33]—i.e., when the actor behaves with **gross recklessness**.

4. At common law, intent to cause grievous bodily injury is sufficient to establish "malice aforethought." The MPC does not adopt this approach—instead, it handles such cases under the standard of extreme recklessness.[34]

5. Reckless murder and reckless manslaughter are distinguished by the nature of the risk involved.

6. Reckless manslaughter and negligent homicide are distinguished by the defendant's consciousness of the risk. See *Hernandez* and *Williams* below.

7. Ordinary (i.e., civil) negligence is generally not sufficient to establish criminal liability, although some states allow it. Generally gross negligence is required.

---
[33] Casebook p. 303.
[34] Casebook p. 304.

4.2.3.1 Implied Malice: *People v. Knoller*

The Supreme Court of California held that implied malice requires awareness of a risk of death, not just serious bodily harm.

1. Defendants came into possession of two large, aggressive Presa Canario dogs. They'd been warned repeatedly about the dogs' dangerously aggressive behavior. The dogs killed a woman in the hallway of the defendants' apartment building.

2. The trial court held that a murder charge required conduct involving "a high probability of resulting in the death of another." The jury found the defendants guilty. The court ordered a new trial.

3. The appellate court granted defendants' motion for a new trial on the grounds that Knoller did not know that her conduct involved a high probability of death. The appellate court reversed the order for a new trial, holding that the standard for second-degree murder should be "conscious disregard of the risk of serious bodily injury to another," rather than a high probability of death.

4. The Supreme Court of California focused on the issue of implied malice as an element of murder. It uses two definitions of implied malice: (1) the *Thomas* test: "wanton disregard for human life, and (2) the *Phillips* test: "conscious disregard for human life." The tests articulate the same standard, but the court prefers the second for clarity.

5. The Supreme Court reversed the appellate court, holding that **implied malice requires awareness of a risk of death, not just serious bodily harm**. It also held that the trial court erred in its interpretation of the test. The trial court held the awareness of a high probability of death to be a subjective perception, but it's actually an objective standard. The subjective component is that the defendant must have acted with "conscious disregard for human life." (Not all jurisdictions require conscious disregard to establish implied malice.)

4.2.3.2 Proving Negligence: *State v. Hernandez*

To prove negligence, the prosecution must show that the defendant was unaware of a substantial and unjustifiable risk. If the defendant was aware of the risk, the mental state is recklessness, not negligence.

1. The defendant killed a woman while he was driving drunk. The trial court convicted him of involuntary manslaughter. The issue on appeal was whether stickers and pins inside the car with "drinking slogans"—"The more I drink the better you look," etc.—were admissible evidence to help establish the elements of involuntary manslaughter, which the

relevant Missouri statute (deriving from the MPC) defined as (1) criminal negligence and (2) resulting death. Criminal negligence is the culpable failure to perceive a substantial and unjustifiable risk.

2. The government introduced the slogans as evidence that the defendant was aware of the risk of driving drunk. But this was a prosecutorial error, because the statute only criminalizes negligence, and if the defendant had been aware of the risk, he could not have acted negligently (though he may have acted recklessly). Therefore, the evidence was inadmissible in the state's attempt to prove the elements of involuntary manslaughter. (The prosecution probably could have proved second-degree murder based on recklessness.)

3. The appellate court held that the slogans served only to illustrate the defendant's character. Reputation and character testimony were inadmissible here. Reversed.

4. The dissent argued that at least three of the slogans indicated that alcohol can impair perception, and that the defendant therefore should have been aware of the substantial risks involved with drinking and driving. It also suggested that the defendant's intoxication might have prevented him from perceiving the risk.

4.2.3.3 Omissions and Negligence: *State v. Williams*

Omissions can constitute negligence. The typical standard for negligent homicide is gross negligence, not ordinary negligence. Theorists contest the justification of punishment for negligent homicide.

1. The defendants' infant child died when they failed to seek medical attention for a tooth infection that became a gangrenous abscess.

2. **At common law, involuntary manslaughter required gross negligence, not just ordinary negligence.** Washington State law, however, only required ordinary negligence.

3. The trial court found the defendants guilty of involuntary manslaughter. The appellate court affirmed.

4. At common law, the defendants likely would not have been convicted of manslaughter.

5. The appellate court found negligence.

6. Washington redrafted its code in 1975. Today, "[c]riminal homicide convictions on the basis of ordinary negligence are nearly non-existent."

7. Is it appropriate to punish negligent homicide?

(a) The utilitarian argument against punishment is that negligent actors cannot be deterred. The MPC drafters rejected this argument, arguing that the threat of deterrence encourages people to act with greater care.

(b) The retributivist argument is that an actor cannot be morally culpable for actions that he does not know he is taking. Stephen Garvey argues that culpability exists in the failure to exercise self-control "over desires that influence the formation and awareness of one's beliefs." Jerome Hall argues that blame is sometimes appropriate in response to negligence, but punishment is not.[35]

4.2.4 Felony-Murder

1. **Felony-murder rule**: "...one is guilty of murder if a death results from conduct during the commission or attempted commission of any felony."[36] Rationales:

   (a) Deterrence: encourage criminals to commit felonies more safely.

   (b) Transferred intent: intent to commit the felony implies intent to commit the homicide.

   (c) Retribution: the defendant's culpability for committing the felony demonstrates an evil mind.

   (d) General culpability.

2. The rule can typically only be invoked for **inherently dangerous felonies**.

3. **Enumerated felonies**: if the felony is enumerated in statute, the homicide is first-degree murder. All others are second-degree.

4. **The MPC does not identify felony-murder as a separate offense.** Instead, offenses that would have triggered the felony-murder rule at common law would likely fall under reckless murder under the MPC. The proliferation of statutory (*malum prohibitem*) felonies led the MPC to **enumerate the specific felonies that can constitute the bases for reckless murder.**[37]

5. **Independent felony (or merger) limitation**: the felony murder rule only applies if the felony is independent of the homicide. Assaultive felonies (those that are "on the road" to homicide) do not trigger the felony-murder rule. Rationales:

   (a) The limitation prevents every felonious assault that results in homicide from being punished as second-degree murder.

---

[35] Casebook pp. 312–13.
[36] ALI Commentary to MPC § 210.2, from *Understanding Criminal Law* p. 510.
[37] The enumerated felonies in the MPC are "robbery, rape or deviate sexual intercourse by force or threat of force, arson, burglary, kidnapping or felonious escape." MPC § 210.2(1)(b), Casebook p. 1000.

4 HOMICIDE

(b) If A negligently kills B, A would be guilty of negligent homicide. Negligent homicide is itself a felony. If the felony-murder rule applied, A would be guilty of murder, and **the crime of negligent homicide would evaporate.** The same is true for voluntary manslaughter (e.g., with provocation).

(c) If the predicate felony is assaultive, **it cannot logically be done more safely.**

6. *Res gestae* **requirement**: the felony-murder rule only applies when a killing occurs during the commission or attempted commission of a felony (which includes any proximate causal relationship).

7. You cannot attempt to commit felony murder.

8. At common law, any felony was punishable by death.

9. At common law, any homicide committed while committing (or attempting to commit) one of several enumerated felonies was considered murder. The homicide was a strict liability offense.

10. Most felony murders could also be charged as depraved heard murder. The felony-murder rule is easier for prosecutors because it allows them to prove murder without establishing mens rea. Some argue that it establishes strict liability for homicides that occur during the commission of a felony, while others hold that committing a felony constitutes implied malice.

4.2.4.1 Applying the Felony-Murder Rule: *People v. Fuller*

The felony-murder rule is harsh.

1. The defendant had been breaking into cars in a parking lot when the police noticed him, and a chase ensued. He accidentally killed a driver while involved in a high speed car chase.

2. The Court of Appeal ruled that the trial court had erred in striking the first-degree murder count. The appellate court allowed the prosecution for first-degree murder under the felony-murder rule—but it noted that if it were "starting from a clean slate," it would not allow the prosecution because the original felony, burglary, was not dangerous to human life.

4.2.4.2 Roth and Sundby, "The Felony-Murder Rule"

1. The US is the only western country that recognizes the felony-murder rule.

2. The rule is meant to (1) deter accidental killings during felonies as well as (2) the felonies themselves. On (1), how can you deter an unintentional act? On (2), there is doubt that stricter punishments deter serious crimes,

and it makes more sense to punish the intended conduct (e.g., carrying a deadly weapon) rather than the unintended killing. It may also creative perverse incentives to commit homicide during the commission of a felony.

3. Transferred intent is not a valid justification for the felony murder rule because of the differences in mens rea for the felony and for murder.

4. Justifying a murder charge on a retributivist justification is a regression to the primitive "evil mind" theory of common law, and it defies the principle of proportional punishment.

4.2.4.3 Crump and Crump, "In Defense of the Felony-Murder Doctrine"

1. "Felony-murder reflects a social judgment" that felonies involving killing are more serious than non-lethal felonies.

2. The rule distinguishes crimes that cause death, thereby "reinforcing the reverence for human life."

3. Core disagreement with Roth and Sundby: punishing negligent killings *can* deter future negligence. Also, felons who killed intentionally might testify that the killings were accidental; the felony-murder rule denies them this defense.

4. A clear felony-murder rule is less confusing to juries, so it leads to more consistent results. Also, by simplifying the questions involved, it makes administration more efficient.

4.2.4.4 Tomkovicz, "The Endurance of the Felony-Murder Rule"

1. Restricting the felony-murder rule to certain types of felonies enhances its fairness, helping the doctrine survive.

4.2.4.5 Inherently Dangerous Felonies: *People v. Howard*

The felony-murder rule is limited to inherently dangerous felonies.

1. The defendant was driving a stolen car without a rear license plate. A chase ensued when police tried to pull him over. During the chase, the defendant hit and killed another driver.

2. The trial jury convicted the defendant of second-degree murder. The appellate court affirmed, rejecting the defendant's claim that he could not be charged with second-degree murder because of California precedent rejecting the felony-murder rule for felonies that are not inherently dangerous.

3. The California Supreme Court looked at the statute defining high-speed chases.[38] It noted that in 1996, the legislature significantly broadened the statutory definition of "willful or wanton disregard for the safety of persons or property" to include any flight from a police officer involving three traffic violations. It concluded that a violation of this statute could result from violating a few minor traffic rules, and therefore any violating "is not, in the abstract, inherently dangerous to human life." Therefore, the prosecution could not rely on the felony-murder rule. Reversed.

4. Brown, concurring and dissenting: this interpretation of the statute defies common sense. The conviction should be overturned, but only because the felony-murder rule should be removed entirely.

5. Baxter, dissenting: "there is no doubt that the defendant committed exactly the reckless endangerment of human life forbidden by the statute."

4.2.4.6 Independent Felony (or Merger) Limitation: *People v. Smith*

If the homicide occurred "on the road" to the predicate felony, the felony murder rule does not apply.

1. Defendant was abusing her child, who accidentally fell, hit her head, and died of respiratory arrest. The predicate felony was child abuse. The trial court applied the felony murder rule to convict her of second-degree murder.

2. *People v. Ireland*: "We therefore hold that a second-degree felony-murder instruction may not properly be given when it is based upon a felony which is an integral part of the homicide and which the evidence produced by the prosecution shows to be an offense included in fact within the offense charged."[39]

3. *People v. Wilson*: The felony-murder rule cannot be applied to cases where the action would not be felonious but for the assault, and the assault is an integral part of the homicide.

4. *People v. Sears*: If assault is intended against one person but results in the accidental killing of another, the felony-murder rule should not apply (because it would carry harsher punishments than if the intended victim was killed, in which case the felony-murder rule would not not apply).

5. *People v. Burton*: The felony-murder rule can apply if the underlying violent action was committed with an "independent felonious purpose." For instance, in an armed robbery case where an accidental killing results, the rule applies because the underlying purpose was to rob, not to assault.

---

[38] § 2800.2, Casebook p. 329.
[39] Casebook p. 335.

4 HOMICIDE

6. The felony-murder rule does not apply in this case. Reversed.

4.2.4.7 Liability for a Non-Felon's Actions: *State v. Sophophone*

The felony-murder rule does not apply when a law enforcement officer causes the death.

1. The defendant and three accomplices broke into a house. The police arrived and shot one of the accomplices. The defendant was charged, among other things, with felony-murder. The trial court convicted him on all counts.

2. Under Kansas state law, aggravated burglary counted as one of the inherently dangerous felonies that triggers the felony-murder rule.

3. The defendant argued that he was in custody at the time of his accomplice's death and cannot therefore be held liable.

4. The two issues in question were (1) "whether the felony-murder rule should apply when the fatal act is performed by a non-felon" and (2) when the felony stopped. There are two approaches:

    (a) **Agency approach** (the majority rule): The felony-murder rule does not apply when the person who causes the death is a non-felon. The killing was the result of actions contrary to the intentions of the felon.

    (b) **Proximate causation approach**: The felony-murder rule applies. A felon is responsible for the consequences of the actions he sets in motion.

5. ***Res gestae*** ("things done"): The felony-murder rule applies when a killing occurs during the commission (or attempted commission) of a felony. Most courts also apply it in the aftermath, e.g., during a getaway.

6. There must also be causal relationship between the death and the felony. The cause must be proximate.

7. The court holds that the rule does not apply. "...we believe that making one criminally responsible for the lawful acts of a law enforcement officer is not the intent of the felony-murder statute as it is currently written."[40]

8. Dissent: nothing in the statute requires the court to adopt the "agency" approach. "This set of events could have very easily resulted in the death of a law enforcement officer, and in my opinion this is exactly the type of case the legislature had in mind when it adopted the felony-murder rule."[41]

---
[40] Casebook p. 340.
[41] Casebook p. 341.

4.2.4.8 Misdemeanor Manslaughter

1. "An unintended homicide that occurs during the commission of an unlawful act not amounting to a felony constitutes common law involuntary manslaughter."[42]

2. Manslaughter convictions have been upheld in cases where the act is morally culpable but not technically criminal—e.g., someone attempted to commit suicide with a gun, someone attempted to intervene, and the one who intervened was accidentally shot and killed.

3. Not all jurisdictions apply the misdemeanor manslaughter rule, and some only apply it for *malum in se* misdemeanors.

4. The MPC does not follow the misdemeanor manslaughter rule because it's too harsh.

---

[42] Casebook p. 343

§ 5 Rape

5.1 Overview

1. At common law, rape was defined as "unlawful carnal knowledge of a woman [not the defendant's wife] **forcibly** and **against her will**."[43]

2. 32% of rapes were reported to law enforcement in 1994 and 1995.[44]

3. 91% of victims were female.[45] (MPC § 213.1 defines rape only as male-against-female.)

4. 8% of forcible rapes reported in 1995 turned out to be unfounded.[46]

5. Susan Estrich: rape law exposes the sexism of the law.

6. Two frameworks for understanding the crime of rape: (1) a crime of violence and (2) a crime against sexual autonomy.[47]

7. Rape is widely believed to be underreported because of (1) the sensitivity of the issue, which makes it hard to bring up, and (2) the difficulty of proof in many cases.

8. The force requirement may have developed to guard against false claims of rape as defenses to fornication and adultery.

9. **Competing definitions of force**: (1) force used to overcome lack of consent or (2) any amount of sexual touching brought about involuntarily.[48] The threat of serious physical harm can satisfy the force requirement.

10. Mens rea is more difficult to establish without the force requirement.

11. The MPC abolished criminal sexual offenses between consenting adults (e.g., sodomy).

12. Rape law has been widely reformed to (1) eliminate the resistance requirement, (2) allow penetration to suffice for the force requirement, and (3) eliminate the spouse rape exemption.

13. Can you be raped, but not by a rapist?

---

[43] Blackstone, 4 Commentaries on the Laws of England 210.
[44] Casebook p. 385.
[45] Casebook p. 386.
[46] Casebook p. 387.
[47] Casebook p. 391.
[48] Casebook p. 437.

5 RAPE

5.1.1 Annette Gordon Reed, *Celia's Case*

1. A white male landowner bought Celia, a female slave, and treated her as a concubine. She eventually decided to stand up to his advances and ended up killing him by hitting him on the head. She stood trial and was put to death.

5.1.2 C. Vann Woodward, Review of *Scottsboro: A Tragedy of the American South*

1. Two white women falsely accused the nine Scottsboro Boys of rape. All were convicted and sentenced. Eventually, all were exonerated.

5.1.3 NY Times Obituary for Ruth Schut

1. A note on the death of one of the two accusers of the Scottsboro Boys. She later recanted her accusations.

5.2 Forcible Rape

1. Some jurisdictions require (or required) the victim to forcibly resist for the defendant to be convicted of rape. See *Alston* below.

2. The forcible resistance requirement has been seriously questioned. See *Rusk* below. Critiques:
   (a) It conflates the force and non-consent elements.
   (b) It emphasizes the victim's conduct and deemphasizes the defendant's conduct.
   (c) The victim's resistance could further compromise the victim's safety.
   (d) Resistance is not always the immediate response to unwanted advances.

3. **Threats of force can be sufficient** to meet the force requirement—e.g., brandishing a knife. The victim need not forcibly resist.

4. Failure to obtain **affirmative assent** can be enough to convict for rape in some jurisdictions. Others require the defendant to show reasonable belief in consent.

5. In some jurisdictions, the force needed for penetration can meet the force requirement. See *M.T.S.* below.

6. The **spouse rape exemption** has been largely dismissed. See *Liberta* below. Its rationales included:
   (a) Promotion of marital harmony.
   (b) Preservation of marital privacy.

(c) Encourage reconciliation between spouses.

(d) Limit opportunities to fabricate rape charges for divorce proceedings.

5.2.1 The Force Requirement: *State v. Alston*

Some jurisdiction require (or required) the victim to forcibly resist for the defendant to be convicted of rape.

1. Alston and Brown were in a semi-abusive relationship. She broke it off. Then, one day, he coerced her to come to a friend's house. She did not forcibly resist his sexual advances. Later that day, she filed a police complaint.

2. The trial court convicted the defendant of second-degree rape.

3. The Supreme Court of North Carolina reasoned that the statutory definition of rape required intercourse to be (1) by force and (2) against the victim's will. The court found no evidence that the victim forcibly resisted. It overturned the conviction.

4. Susan Estrich: The victim was not forced to engage in sex, but did so against her will. "To say that there is no 'force' in such a situation is to create a gulf between power and force, and to define the latter solely in schoolboy terms."[49]

5. Vivian Berger: It's not clear that this was actually a rape. Overprotecting women "risks enfeebling instead of empowering."[50]

5.2.2 Questioning the Force Requirement: *Rusk v. State*

Judge Wilner's dissent rails against the force requirement.

1. The victim met the defendant at bar. She drove him home. She did not want to go into his apartment, but he took her car keys out of her ignition, and she followed him out of fear. They had sex and she did not resist.

2. The trial court convicted him of rape. He argued on appeal that there was insufficient evidence for conviction. The Court of Special Appeals of Maryland here reversed.

3. Judge Wilner, dissenting, argues that lack of resistance is not consent:

    (a) The court inappropriately substituted its judgement for the jury's.

    (b) The court's reasoning requires the victim to either (1) resist, risking physical harm or death, or (2) "be termed a willing partner."[51]

---

[49] Casebook p. 409
[50] Casebook p. 410.
[51] Casebook p. 414.

5 RAPE

(c) The defendant's actions demonstrate the requisite threat of force to prove robbery. Why doesn't it prove rape?

(d) Rape victims who resist are more likely to be injured than those who don't.[52]

(e) Courts can look to factors other than physical resistance, e.g., reasonable expressions of fear.

5.2.3 Removing the Force Requirement: *State v. Rusk*

The court here abandoned the requirement. The dissent's fear might be based on the racial subtext—e.g., in Scottsboro the accused were wrongly convicted, and a force requirement might have given some protection.

1. The Court of Appeals of Maryland agreed with Judge Wilner's dissent (above). The victim's apprehension of fear "was plainly a question of fact for the jury." Remanded for a new trial.

2. Judge Cole, dissenting: words expressing fear "do not transform a seducer into a rapist." Rape is a crime of violence. The victim "must resist unless the defendant has objectively manifested his intent to use physical force to accomplish is purpose."

5.2.4 Susan Anger, *The Incident*

1. Anger writes about her rape and why she did not forcibly resist.

5.2.5 Acquaintance Rape: *State of New Jersey in the Interest of M.T.S.*

The prosecution only needs to show force required for penetration, not additional physical force. Rape is proven if there was force and lack of consent.

1. Fifteen-year-old C.G. lived in a house with nine other people, including seventeen-year-old M.T.S. C.G. testified that she woke up to find M.T.S. on top of her and sexually penetrating her. She slapped him and "he jumped right off."[53] According to M.T.S., they briefly had consensual sex before she pushed him off and "he hopped off right away." "The court did not fully credit either teenager's testimony."[54]

2. The trial court found him guilty of sexual assault. The appellate court reversed, holding that rape required "some level of force more than that necessary to accomplish the penetration."[55]

---

[52]Casebook pp. 415–416.
[53]Casebook p. 436.
[54]Casebook p. 435.
[55]Casebook p. 435.

5 RAPE

3. The Supreme Court of New Jersey held that the force requirement did not call for physical force beyond the force needed for penetration. Rape is proven if there is (1) force needed for penetration and (2) lack of consent. Both elements were present here. Reversed.

4. New Jersey reframed rape as a crime of violence, focusing on the defendant's actions, not the victim's. This aligns with the law's analysis of other violent crimes—e.g., you don't require a victim's resistance in robbery.

5.2.6 Ending Wife Rape: *People v. Liberta*

1. The New York Supreme Court squarely rejected the spouse exemption for rape. "Among the recent decisions in this country addressing the marital exemption, only one court has concluded that there is a rational basis for it.... We agree with the other courts which have analyzed the exemption, which have been unable to find any present justification for it.... [T]he marital exemption...lacks a rational basis, and therefore violates the equal protection clauses of both the Federal and State Constitutions."

5.2.7 Margaret Mitchell, *Gone With the Wind*

1. An excerpt from the controversial "rape of Scarlett" where forcible sex becomes consensual.

5.2.8 Male Rape: *State v. Gounagias*

1. An instance of a male rape victim.

5.3 Mens Rea

5.3.1 Mistake of Fact: *People v. Williams*

Mistake of fact regarding consent is available as a defense when (1) the defendant believed in good faith that there was consent and (2) the mistake was reasonable.

1. The defendant and the victim went to a hotel room to watch TV, according to the victim. They had sex, but their factual accounts differ significantly. The defendant claimed that it was consensual, but that afterwards the victim said she would claim rape unless he gave her $50. The victim claimed it was forcible non-consensual sex.

2. The trial court did not instruct the jury on a mistaken belief of consent. It convicted the defendant of forcible rape and false imprisonment.

3. The Court of Appeal reversed.

4. Here, the Supreme Court of California based its understanding of mistake of fact in rape cases on *People v. Mayberry*. A successful *Mayberry* defense requires (1) a good faith belief in the mistaken fact and (2) that the mistake

5 RAPE

was reasonable. The jury can only receive instruction on the defense when there is "substantial evidence" to support it.

5. For the defense to be available, there must have been substantial evidence of equivocal conduct. The court here found that (1) there was no evidence of equivocal conduct on the part of the victim and (2) that the defendant's argument sought to prove actual consent, not a reasonable mistake of consent. It reversed the appellate court.

6. Mosk, concurring: first, the majority's interpretation of the *Mayberry* rule is illogical. It would require the defendant to take the position that he was mistaken about consent, and therefore that there was no consent. Second, "equivocal conduct" from the victim is not necessary. Requiring it means that in cases where the facts are in dispute, such as this one, the jury must completely credit the victim's account and discredit the defendant's.

7. Kennard, concurring: there are three fact patterns where force *and* consent are present: (1) where the amount of force is "slight," (2) where the victim consents to the use of force, and (3) where enough time has passed between the threat of force and the act of intercourse so that the defendant could reasonably believed that the victim's participation was not coerced.[56]. The *Mayberry* defense should only be available in these three cases.

5.4 Statutory Rape

1. Policy goals of statutory rape laws:

    (a) Protect children.

    (b) Provide recourse for rape victims who could not prove force or resistance.

2. Criticisms:

    (a) Criminalizes consensual activity.

    (b) Limits sexual autonomy.

    (c) May be used in a discriminatory way to prosecute teenagers.

3. Reforms:

    (a) Limit liability for defendants who are close in age to victims.

    (b) Recognizing mistake of fact regarding the victim's age as a defense.

    (c) Selective prosecution.

4. Some jurisdictions define statutory rape as a strict liability offense. In those cases, mistake of fact is not a defense.

---

[56]Casebook p. 460

5.4.1 *State v. Garnett*

A quick history of statutory rape law.

1. Statutory rape law as oppressive: young females are presumed "too innocent and naive to understand the implications and nature of her act." The male is presumed criminally responsible—even in cases where he himself might be young and naive.[57]

2. Early reforms: Victorian feminists urged statutory rape laws to curb the spread of venereal disease and protect young females from sexual abuse.[58]

3. 1970s reforms: statutory rape laws seen as restrictions on sexual autonomy. Most jurisdictions made statutory rape gender neutral. Many have advocated for abolishing it entirely.[59]

4. *Michael M. v. Superior Court of Sonoma County*: US Supreme Court upheld gender-specific statutory rape laws on the basis of deterring teenage pregnancy.

5.4.2 Equal Protection: *State v. Limon*

Statutes defining different sex crime standards for homosexual and heterosexual acts violate equal protection.

1. The defendant had turned 18 one week before having homosexual intercourse with a 14-year-old. The age gap was less than four years. He was convicted of criminal sodomy and sentenced to 206 months in prison. Under the recent Kansas "Romeo and Juliet" statute, he would have been sentenced to only 13–15 months in prison if the contact had been heterosexual.[60] He argued that the Romeo and Juliet statute violated equal protection because of harsher punishment for homosexuals.

2. The trial court convicted him of criminal sodomy and the appellate court confirmed.

3. The Supreme Court of Kansas considered in detail the possible rationales for the statute. It concluded that there was no rational basis for the law.

4. The court held that the statute violated the equal protection clauses in both the state and federal constitutions. It reversed the conviction and struck the words "and are members of the opposite sex" from the statute.

---

[57] Casebook p. 478–479.
[58] Casebook p. 477.
[59] Casebook p. 478.
[60] p. 1 (WestLaw).

§ 6 Defenses

6.1 Overview

1. A defense is "any set of identifiable conditions or circumstances which may prevent a conviction for an offense."[61]

2. **Failure of proof defense**: negate a required element of the offense—e.g., mistake of fact in a strict liability crime.

3. **Offense modification**: "while the actor has apparently satisfied all the elements of the offense charged, he has not in fact caused the harm or evil sought to be prevented by the statute defining the offense"—e.g., a parent of a kidnapped child pays ransom to the kidnapper, which satisfies the elements of complicity in kidnapping but confers a defense to criminal charges.[62]

4. **Justification**: society tolerates or even encourages the conduct—e.g., burning a field to save a town of 10,000.

5. **Excuse**: the deed may be wrong, but the conditions are such that the actor is not responsible—e.g., the "actor knocks the mailman over the head with a baseball bat because she believes he is coming to surgically implant a radio receiver which will take control of her body."[63]

6. **Nonexculpatory public policy defense**: the act is wrong, but policy reasons dictate a defense—e.g., the statute of limitations.

7. Defenses in the MPC are in § 3.

8. **Justification of the *act*, excuse of the *actor*.**

6.2 Justification

1. Justification focuses on the **act, not the actor**.

2. Justified acts are socially redeemable.

3. Structure of justification defenses: "triggering conditions permit a necessary and proportional response."[64]

    (a) *Triggering conditions*: circumstances that must exist before the actor can act with justification—e.g., an aggressor threatens unjustified harm against a protected interest.

    (b) *Necessary*: the response must be necessary to protect the interest at stake.

---

[61]Casebook p. 480.
[62]Casebook p. 482.
[63]Casebook p. 482.
[64]Casebook p. 497.

6 DEFENSES

(c) *Proportional*: the act must cause harm in reasonable relation to the harm threatened.

4. Where an actor has no option but deadly force to prevent a thief from stealing apples from her orchard, she must sacrifice her apples out of regard to the thief's life.[65]

6.2.1 Self-Defense

1. Self-defense is the most common justification defense.

2. Common law elements of self-defense (all are necessary):

    (a) An honest and reasonable fear of death or great bodily harm.

    (b) An imminent and unlawful threat.

    (c) A proportional response to the threat.

    (d) The defendant must not have been the initial aggressor.

    (e) (Some jurisdictions impose a duty on the defendant to retreat, except in his own home.)

3. MPC:

    (a) *Subjectivity*: the actor must believe the use of force is necessary. Reasonableness is not required.[66]

    (b) *"Force is immediately necessary" replaces "imminent threat"*: shifts from threat to necessity of force (e.g., allows a battered spouse to shoot the abuser while the abuser sleeps—see *Norman* below).

    (c) *Expands castle doctrine* to include place of work.

    (d) As at common law, the MPC does not allow the defense if the defendant provoked the use of force against himself by using serious force, or if he can safely retreat (except at home or at work).

4. The two key differences between common law and the MPC are **objectively vs. subjectively reasonable** requirement and the **immediately necessary vs. imminent harm** requirement.

5. Critiques of self-defense (from Murray):

    (a) In recent years, critics have argued that the law of self-defense is insufficiently attentive to the physical (and other) differences between men and women.

    (b) Some have argued that the emphasis on the reasonable man's response makes the male experience the legal default.

---

[65]Casebook p. 497.
[66]MPC § 3.09(2).

6 DEFENSES 57

(c) In this vein, the objective standard is said to preclude defensive actions that are objectively unreasonable, but that are completely reasonable in light of the defendant's idiosyncratic circumstances.

(d) Further, many have argued that the doctrine's imminence requirement precludes the use of the defense in domestic violence situations.

(e) The MPC and its more subjective standards might appear to be more attuned to these sorts of criticisms than the common law approach.

6. **Imperfect self-defense** mitigates to manslaughter. Two versions:

   (a) First: a nondeadly aggressor who is the victim of a deadly atttack must retreat to a place of complete safety before using deadly force. Otherwise, his defense is considered imperfect.

   (b) Second: unreasonable belief that the killing in self-defense was justified.[67]

   (c) MPC: the defendant is justified in using deadly force if he subjectively believed that it was necessary. However, if he was reckless or negligent regarding the facts relating to his conduct, he cannot use the defense for crimes for which recklessness or negligence establish culpability (e.g., he cannot raise self-defense against the charge of negligent homicide).[68]

6.2.1.1 Self-Defense and Provocation: *United States v. Peterson*

Self-defense is usually not available to a defendant to provokes or is the aggressor in it. The castle doctrine is only available to a defendant who is without fault in bringing on the conflict.

1. The victim was stealing the windshield wipers from the defendant's car. The defendant got a pistol and said, "If you move, I will shoot." The victim picked up a wrench and walked toward the defendant with the wrench raised. The defendant told him to "not take another step." The victim kept walking and defendant shot him in the face, killing him instantly.

2. The trial court indicted him for second-degree murder and the jury convicted him of manslaughter.

3. The defendant argued that two jury instructions were erroneous: (1) on whether he was the aggressor in the altercation before the homicide, and (2) on whether he could have retreated without jeopardizing his safety.

4. The defendant argued that the killing was excusable.

5. At common law, there would be no excuse defense.

---

[67]Understanding Criminal Law pp. 232–33.
[68]MPC § 3.09(2) and Understanding Criminal Law p. 253.

6. On the first point, the court found that "the evidence plainly presented an issue of fact as to whether Peterson's conduct was an invitation to and provocation of the encounter which ended in the fatal shot."[69]

7. On the second point, the court found that the instruction on retreat was proper. The defendant countered that the "castle" doctrine does not require a defendant to retreat from his own house. The court rejected this argument on the grounds that the doctrine "can be invoked only by one who is without fault in bringing the conflict on."[70]

8. Affirmed.

6.2.1.2 Self-Defense and Reasonable Belief: *People v. Goetz*

In New York, to successfully claim self-defense a defendant must have acted as a reasonable person would have acted.

1. Goetz shot several youths on a New York City subway after they approached him and asked for money.

2. The trial court indicted Goetz for attempted murder, assault, and weapons possession. It dismissed the case on erroneous jury instructions on the defense of justification. It found that the prosecutor erred in instructing jurors to consider how a reasonable man would have acted under the circumstances. The statutory test for justification should be "wholly subjective."[71]

3. Appellate court: affirmed dismissal.[72]

4. The prosecutor, the trial court, and a plurality of the appellate court read the New York justification statute to mean that the defendant's belief must have been "reasonable to him." This is consistent with the MPC, on which the NY criminal statutory reforms of 1961 were based.

5. However, the court here argued that the NY statute does not follow the MPC. The legislature intended to keep the objective reasonableness requirement.

6. Court of Appeals reversed and reinstated the indictments.

6.2.1.3 Abused Spouse Syndrome: *State v. Norman*

Self-defense for battered spouses presents a jury question.

---
[69] p. 504.
[70] Casebook p. 505.
[71] Casebook p. 513.
[72] Casebook p. 513.

6 DEFENSES

1. J.T. Norman was found dead from two gunshot wounds to the head. The defendant, his wife, told police that he had been beating her all day and that she shot him while he slept. The trial court refused to grant an acquittal on self-defense.

2. Multiple experts testified that Mrs. Norman suffered from abused spouse syndrome and did not leave because she thought escape was completely impossible. The experts testified that she believed killing her husband while he slept was necessary.

3. The court held that she "believed killing the victim was necessary to avoid being killed."[73] The evidence was sufficient to send the question of self-defense to the jury. Reversed.

6.2.1.4 Imminence: *State v. Norman*

Self-defense requires an imminent, not potential, threat of harm.

1. On appeal from the appellate court case (above), the North Carolina Supreme Court reversed, holding that self-defense requires a threat of *imminent* death or great bodily harm. The defendant "had ample time and opportunity to resort to other means of prevent further abuse of her husband."[74]

2. If the appellate court's approach were allowed, "[h]omicidal self-help would then become a lawful solution" for battered spouses.[75]

6.2.2 Necessity

1. Recognized in around twenty jurisdictions.

2. Elements of the common law necessity defense (compare to MPC § 3.02, below):

    (a) Clear and imminent danger.

    (b) Actor expects, as a reasonable person, that his action will abate the danger.

    (c) No legal way to avert the danger.

    (d) The harm caused by violating the law is less than the harm to be avoided.

    (e) The defense is not prohibited by statute.

    (f) "Clean hands": defendant must not have substantially contributed to the emergency.

---

[73] Casebook p. 536.
[74] Casebook p. 538.
[75] Casebook p. 539.

3. The defendant's actions are evaluated in terms of the harm that was reasonably foreseeable at the time, rather than the harm that actually occurred.

4. Common (but not universal) limitations on the necessity defense:

    (a) Preclusion by legislature.

    (b) "Clean hands" requirement.

    (c) Danger must have been created by a force of nature.

    (d) Must be used to protect persons or property (and not, say, economic interests).

5. Why have the necessity defense?

    (a) Utilitarianism: maximize social welfare.

    (b) Retributivism: an actor cannot be culpable if the goal is to avoid harm.

6.2.2.1 MPC § 3.02 ("Choice of Evils") and ALI Commentary

- (1) Conduct to avoid harm is justified if:
    - (a) The harm avoided is greater than the harm caused.
    - (b) There are no explicit exceptions for this particular situation.
    - (c) There is no legislative purpose to exclude the claimed justification.

- (2) If the actor recklessly or negligently caused the situation, the justification offense cannot be used to defend against an offense for which recklessness or negligence establishes culpability.

- **MPC differences from common law necessity**:

    1. Harm need not be imminent.
    2. No "clean hands" requirement, i.e., the defendant can have contributed to the emergency.
    3. No mention of homicide.
    4. No mention of economic interests vs. personal interests. Arguably it would allow the necessity defense for protection of economic interests.
    5. Does not permit the defense where (1) the defendant's belief in the danger was negligent or reckless and (2) the mental state required for the offense was recklessness or negligence.[76]

---

[76]MPC § 3.02(2).

6.2.2.2 Emergencies: *Nelson v. State*

You can appropriate property in emergencies, but only if a reasonable person would believe the situation constituted an emergency.

1. Nelson's truck became bogged down. He and two companions took a dump truck from the Highway Department Yard to help pull out the truck, and it also got stuck. A man named Curly helped them take a front-end loader from the yard, which also got stuck.

2. The trial court and appellate court affirmed convictions of reckless destruction of personal property and joyriding.

3. Nelson argued that the jury instruction on the necessity defense should have been based on a subjective interpretation of the emergency situation. The court here agreed, but held that there was not a reasonable apprehension of emergency (since the truck remained stable for 12 hours and one of the actors slept in it). Moreover, there were lawful alternatives. Affirmed.

6.2.2.3 Civil Disobedience: *United States v. Schoon*

Laws and policies do not constitute the types of harms that allow for the necessity defense.

1. The three defendants disrupted an IRS office out of protest of US policies in El Salvador. The district court denied them the necessity defense.

2. There are four elements of the necessity defense:

    (a) Actors chose the lesser evil.
    (b) They acted to prevent imminent harm.
    (c) They "reasonably anticipated a direct causal relationship between their conduct and the harm to be averted."[77]
    (d) They had no legal alternatives.

3. The necessity defense is not available if any of the four elements are lacking.

4. The court distinguished between indirect and direct civil disobedience. This case involved indirect civil disobedience.

5. Necessity is a utilitarian defense because it aims to maximize social welfare.

6. The court reasoned:

---

[77] Casebook p. 567.

6 DEFENSES

(a) Balance of harms: law or policy "cannot constitute a legally cognizable harm."

(b) Causal relationship: indirect civil disobedience is "unlikely to abate the evil."

(c) Legal alternatives: "legal alternatives will never be deemed exhausted when the harm can be mitigated by congressional action."[78]

7. Affirmed.

8. Judge Fernandez, concurring: "I am not so sure that this defense of justification should be grounded on utilitarian theory alone."

6.2.2.4 *The Queen v. Dudley and Stephens*

1. Facts: see p. 6.

2. Was the killing of Richard Parker necessary and justified, or was it murder?

3. Bracton and Hale: the only justified killing is in self-defense.

4. *United States v. Holmes*: If killing some would save others, and there is no imminent danger, those to die must be chosen by lot.

5. Bacon: contradicting Hale—if you're on a lifeboat, and another passenger would sink it, you can justifiably push him away.

6. The court here found murder. "...a man has no right to declare temptation to be an excuse, though he might himself have yielded to it..."[79]

6.3 Excuse

1. Focuses on the **actor, not the act**.

2. Theories of excuse:

    (a) **Utilitarian**: Bentham: "identify situations in which conduct is nondeterrable, so that punishment would be so much unnecessary evil." Hart: excuses maximize the effect of a person's choices within the framework of coercive law.

    (b) **Causation**: "a person should not be blamed for her conduct if it was caused by factors outside her control."[80]

    (c) **Character**: punishment should be proportional to a wrongdoer's moral desert, and moral desert should be measured by the actor's overall character. Or: a person should not be blamed for her conduct in circumstances where bad character cannot be inferred from the conduct.

---
[78] Casebook p. 570.
[79] Casebook p. 575.
[80] Casebook p. 581.

6 DEFENSES

(d) **Free Choice**: people should only be punished for actions they freely committed. An actor is free if he has the capacity and opportunity to (1) understand the facts, (2) appreciate that the conduct violates society's mores, and (3) conform her conduct to the dictates of the law.[81]

6.3.1 Duress

1. **Elements of the duress defense:**

   (a) Another person threatened to kill or seriously injure the defendant or a third party (usually a close relative) unless the defendant commit the offense.

   (b) The defendant reasonably believed the threat was genuine.

   (c) The threat was "present, imminent, and impending" at the time of the criminal act.

   (d) There was no reasonable escape from the threat except through compliance.

   (e) The defendant was not at fault in exposing himself to the threat.

   (f) The defense is not available in homicide cases.

2. MPC duress:[82]: "It is an affirmative defense that the actor was engaged in the conduct charged to constitute an offense because he was coerced to do so by the use of, or a threat to use, unlawful force against his person or the person of another, that a person of reasonable firmness in his situation would have been unable to resist."

3. Common law vs. MPC:

   (a) Abandons the deadly force and imminent threat requirements. Instead, it takes the threat and its imminence as factors in evaluating whether person of reasonable firmness under the circumstances would have committed the offense.

   (b) The threat can be to any person, regardless of the defendant's relationship.

   (c) The reasonableness requirement takes into account the defendant's full situation (e.g., prior experiences, emotional condition).

   (d) The MPC *does* allow the duress defense in homicide cases.

---

[81]Casebook p. 582.
[82]MPC § 2.09(1)

6.3.1.1 Coercion to Smuggle Drugs: *United States v. Contento-Pachon*

The duress defense can be available to someone coerced into smuggling drugs.

1. The defendant was coerced into smuggling cocaine into the US.

2. The trial court excluded evidence of duress.

3. The Appellate court here held that there was sufficient evidence of duress to send the factual questions to a jury.

4. There are three elements of duress: (1) immediate threat of death or serious bodily injury, (2) well-grounded fear that the threat will be carried out, and (3) no reasonable opportunity to escape.

5. The necessity defense was not available because the situation was not caused by physical forces and the defendant did not act to promote the general welfare.

6. Coyle, dissenting and concurring: defendant failed to establish the immediacy and inescapability needed for the excuse defense.

6.3.1.2 Duress and Murder: *People v. Anderson*

Duress is never a defense to murder (at least in California).

1. The defendant, a father, was coerced by another father to murder a woman suspected of molesting their children.

2. The defendant argued that he killed under duress.

3. The jury convicted defendant of first-degree murder and kidnapping.

4. A California statute prevents the duress defense for any crime "punishable by death." When the statute was passed, all forms of murder were punishable by death. Now, only first degree murder is punishable by death. The court here chose to retain the original scope. It held that duress is never a defense to murder.

5. The defendant also argued that duress negated the malice necessary to find murder, and therefore the charge should be reduced to manslaughter. The court held that this would require a new form of voluntary manslaughter, and that only the legislature can make this designation.

6. The dissent argued that the statutory language should apply to crimes currently punishable by death, not at the time of the drafting of the original statute.

6.3.2 Intoxication

1. **Voluntary intoxication:**

   (a) Early common law: **Not a defense at common law.** The intoxicated defendant "shall have no privilege by this **voluntarily contracted madness**, but shall have the same judgment as if he were in his right senses."[83]

   (b) Current common law: some jurisdictions only allow voluntary intoxication to mitigate punishment for graded specific intent crimes (but it cannot completely exculpate the defendant). Others allow it to be a completely exculpatory defense for any specific intent crimes.

   (c) *Montana v. Egelhoff*: the Supreme Court held that states can preclude the defendant from using intoxication to negate mens rea without violating due process.

   (d) MPC § 2.08:

   - "[I]ntoxication of the actor is not a defense unless it negatives an element of the offense."
   - When recklessness establishes an element of the offense, if the actor, due to self-induced intoxication, is unaware of a risk of which he would have been unaware had he been sober, such unawareness is immaterial.

2. **Involuntary intoxication:**

   (a) Common law:

   i. Intoxication is involuntary if coerced, the result of an innocent mistake, unexpected from a prescribed medication within the prescribed dose, or "pathological intoxication" (an unforeseen psychotic reaction to a substance).

   ii. Proof of involuntary intoxication can negate the mens rea for both general and specific intent crimes.

   (b) MPC § 2.08(4):

   i. "Intoxication that (a) is not self-induced or (b) is pathological is an affirmative defense if by reason of such intoxication the actor at the time of his conduct lacks substantial capacity either to appreciate its criminality [wrongfulness] or to conform his conduct to the requirements of law."

6.3.2.1 Specific Intent Crimes: *United States v. Veach*

Intoxication is a defense only to specific intent crimes.

---

[83] Sir Matthew Hale.

1. The defendant was drunk and got involved in a car accident. He made death threats against the park rangers who arrested him.

2. The jury convicted him of one count of resisting a federal law enforcement officer and two counts of threatening to assault and murder a law enforcement officer.

3. The court held that intoxication is a defense when it negates the mens rea of a crime.

4. Resisting an officer is a general intent crime, so intoxication is not a defense.

5. Threatening an officer, however, is a specific intent crime, so the defendant should have been allowed to present the defense to a jury.

6.3.3 Insanity

1. Mental illness in medicine is a broad spectrum. Mental illness in law is a binary state. Sometimes, mental illness in medicine is insufficient to establish mental illness in law.

2. Insanity can only be raised for **recognized mental disorders**. Other mental incapacity claims (e.g., inability to form intent because of toxic exposure) fall under diminished capacity.

3. **"Deific decree"**: "God told me to do it," and the actor realized that their conduct was socially unacceptable. The MPC allows this to establish insanity because the he lacked substantial capacity to appreciate wrongfulness. The M'Naghten test does not allow it because the actor knows it is wrong (and so many M'Naghten jurisdictions include specific exceptions for deific decrees, but not for general religious beliefs).

4. **Insanity tests**: see *Johnson* below.

6.3.3.1 *United States v. Freeman*

Insanity is available as an excuse defense.

1. "...none of the three asserted purposes of criminal law—rehabilitation, deterrence, and retribution—is satisfied when the truly irresponsible are punished."[84]

2. The insanity defense aims to "draw a line between the bad and the mad."[85]

---

[84] Casebook p. 616.
[85] Casebook p. 617.

6.3.3.2 State v. Johnson

There are several competing tests for determining whether a defendant qualifies for the insanity defense. The M'Naghten and MPC tests are the most popular. Some jurisdictions only use one prong of M'Naghten.

1. A legal standard has to reflect community values, incorporate scientific understanding, and preserve the factfinder's authority to render a decision.

2. **Right-wrong test**: whether a defendant has "knowledge of good or evil."[86]

3. **M'Naghten rule**: to establish the defense, the defendant must have suffered from a mental disease such that he (1) did "not know the nature and quality of the act he was doing, or (2) if he did know it, that he did not know what he was doing was wrong."[87] Criticisms include:

    (a) It recognizes only cognitive impairments, but not volitional or emotional impairments.

    (b) Its "all-or-nothing approach" requires total incapacity of cognition.

    (c) It severely restricts expert testimony by calling for an ethical judgment.

4. **Irresistable impulse test**: "courts inquire into both the cognitive and volitional components of the defendant's behavior."[88] A person is insane if (1) he acted from an irresistible or uncontrollable impulse, (2) he was unable to choose between right and wrong behavior, and (3) his will was destroyed such that his actions were beyond his control. Criticisms:

    (a) Like M'Naghten, it takes an absolutist view of the capacity to know.

    (b) It suggests that a crime must have been committed "in a sudden and explosive fit."

5. *Durham*/**Product test**: "an accused is not criminally responsible if his unlawful act was the product of a mental disease or mental defect." The main problem was that expert witnesses usurped the jury's function. The DC Court of Appeals, which originally introduced the test in 1954, repealed it in 1972.

6. **MPC/ALI test**: acknowledges that volitional and cognitive impairments are important. MPC § 4.01 allows the insanity defense when (1) because of a mental disease or defect, "the defendant lacked substantial capacity to appreciate the criminality [wrongfulness] of his conduct, and (2) "lacked substantial capacity to conform his conduct to the requirements of law."[89]

---

[86] Casebook p. 619.
[87] Casebook p. 620.
[88] Casebook p. 621.
[89] Casebook p. 622.

7. (The M'Naghten rule has been upheld as constitutional because no test has been widely accepted as the baseline, so employing one test instead of others does not pose a due process issue. It's not yet clear whether abolishing the insanity defense is unconstitutional.[90])

6.3.3.3 Criminality and Wrongfulness: *State v. Wilson*

If the defendant genuinely believed that society would have viewed his actions as criminal but not wrongful, he can claim insanity.

1. Wilson killed Jack Peters because of delusions about mind control. There was no question that he was mentally ill. The question was whether he was criminally insane.

2. The jury rejected his insanity claim and convicted him of murder.

3. The question on appeal was the meaning of "wrongfulness" under Connecticut General Statutes § 53a–13(a) (modeled on MPC § 4.01).

4. Wilson argued that wrongfulness has a moral element, so that the accused is not guilty if he believes his act was not morally wrong, even if he believed it was criminal. The trial court refused to give this instruction.

5. The appellate court addressed two questions: (1) what is the meaning of wrongfulness, and (2) was the defendant's requested instruction necessary in this case?

6. The court noted three features of the MPC definition:

    (a) It includes both a cognitive and a volitional component.

    (b) It focuses on the defendant's appreciation of, not just knowledge of, the wrongfulness of his conduct. This accounts for cases where the defendant is aware of the wrongfulness but is not affected by it.

    (c) It allows legislatures to choose between "criminality" and "wrongfulness."

7. Defendant contended that the insanity defense instructions must define morality in purely personal terms.

8. The state contended that the defendant must be held to morality according to a social standard, unless he lacked the capacity to appreciate the social moral standard.

9. Court found that the state's version "does not sufficiently account for a delusional defendant's own distorted perception of society's moral standards."[91] If the defendant believed that society would not have condemned

---
[90]Casebook pp. 624–25.
[91]Casebook p. 634.

his actions under the circumstances as he understood them, he can claim insanity. If he did not believe that society would accept his actions, however, the defense is not available.

10. The defendant *can* believe that his acts are criminal without believing that they are wrongful.

11. The court held that the defendant presented sufficient evidence for a jury to have found insanity.

12. Justice Katz, concurring: the test as the majority interpreted it might exclude defendants who adhere to a personal code of morality because of their mental illness.

13. Justice McDonald, dissenting: we should not excuse people who kill even though they know society does not condone the killing. The common sense of juries will hopefully mitigate the impact of the majority's ruling. The defendant's conduct showed that he could have been deterred.

6.3.4 Diminished Capacity

1. There are two commmmn law variants of the diminished capacity defense: the **mens rea** and **partial responsibility** variants.

    (a) The **"mens rea" variant**:
        i. If the prosecution cannot prove the mens rea, the defendant must be acquitted. It is a failure of proof defense.
        ii. Claiming no mens rea because of a mental disorder is not the same as claiming legal insanity. The defendant is not claiming partial responsibility, but "straightforwardly denying the prosecution's prima facie case."[92]

    (b) The **"partial responsibility" variant**:
        i. Partial responsibility *is* a form of lesser legal insanity. The defendant claims less culpability and argues he should be convicted of a lesser crime or punished less severely. It is a mitigating excuse defense.

    (c) Limitations on the common law approach: (1) most allow the mens rea variant, but only for specific intent crimes, and (2) a minority allow the partial responsibility variant, but only to mitigate murder to manslaughter.

2. The MPC contains two diminished capacity tests:

    (a) **Mens rea**, § 4.02(1): "Evidence that the defendant suffered from a mental disease or defect is admissible whenever it is relevant to prove that the defendant did or did not have a state of mind which is an element of the offense."

---
[92]Casebook p. 657.

i. Can be used to negate the intent for *any* crime—not just specific intent crimes.

(b) **EMED in manslaughter** (a variant of the common law partial responsibility test), § 210.3(1)(b): "Homicide constitutes manslaughter when: (b) a homicide that would otherwise be murder is committed under the influence of extreme mental or emotional disturbance for which there is a reasonable explanation or excuse."

(c) Both allow capital cases to be mitigated to imprisonment.

3. The California Supreme Court held in several cases that mental illness could negate premeditation, deliberation, and sometimes even malice aforethought. The legislature abolished the defense after the Twinkie Defense affair, so **diminished capacity is no longer a defense in California**. Other jurisdictions also do not recognize it.

4. A rationale for the diminished capacity defense is the **"continuum of competence,"** which allows a defense where the full insanity defense is not available—e.g., the **Twinkie Defense**.

5. States that have adopted the MPC's EMED standard have mostly also adopted the partial responsibility model of diminished capacity.[93]

6.3.4.1 *Clark v. Arizona*

Mental-disease evidence can only be introduced as part of an insanity defense, not a diminished capacity defense—though states may adopt the opposite rule without running afoul of due process.

1. Clark was circling the block in his truck. Officer Moritz responded and Clark shot him. Clark suffered from schizophrenia and had talked about wanting to kill a police officer.

2. Clark claimed mental illness in an attempt to rebut evidence of the mens rea for intentionally or knowingly killing a police officer. The trial court did not allow the defense, holding under the *Mott* rule that only insanity could negate the mens rea and convicting Clark of first-degree murder.

3. The Supreme Court identified three types of evidence: "observation" evidence (e.g., witness testimony), "mental-disease" evidence, and "capacity" evidence (indicating the defendant's capacity for cognition and moral judgment). *Mott* restricted the latter two types.

4. Clark argued that the *Mott* restrictions violated due process.

5. The Court here, Justice Souter, held that mental-disease and capacity evidence can be restricted to their bearing on the insanity defense. It identified several dangers of relying on capacity evidence:

---

[93] Casebook p. 659.

6 DEFENSES

(a) It might mask internal debates in professional psychology about the mental disease.

(b) It could mislead jurors to believe that the defendant lacked certain capacities when in fact he did not.

(c) Expert witnesses might inappropriately substitute their own opinions on capacity for mental-disease diagnoses.

6. Other states are free to adopt the opposite rule.

7. Justice Kennedy, dissenting:

   (a) Clark's evidence of lack of capacity was "critical and reliable."[94]

   (b) "Simply put, knowledge relies on cognition, and cognition can be affected by schizophrenia."

   (c) The issue is not whether mental illness is an excuse, but whether it "made him unaware that he was shooting a police officer."[95]

   (d) The risk of speculative testimony from expert witnesses does not explain why evidence of mental illness can *never* be used.

   (e) The risk of jury confusion is unconvincing because juries constantly deal with complex issues.

   (f) The Court confuses the insanity defense with the question of intent.

   (g) The fact that state and defense experts drew different conclusions about Clark's mental illness made the evidence contested but not misleading.

6.3.5 Infancy

1. Infancy is a capacity defense.

2. Common law: there was a conclusive presumption of incapacity for children under the age of seven. There was a rebuttable presumption of capacity between seven and fourteen. See *Devon T* below.

3. The MPC transfers infancy cases to juvenile courts.[96]

6.3.5.1 *In re Devon T*

There is a presumption of incapacity for young children that diminishes as they get older.

1. The incapacity to distinguish right from wrong in the M'Naghten test is a characteristic of many defenses in addition to insanity—infancy, mental illness and retardation, and involuntary intoxication.

---
[94] Casebook p. 667.
[95] Casebook p. 668.
[96] MPC § 4.10.

2. *Doli capax*: capable of criminal intent. *Doli incapax*: incapable.[97]

3. The juvenile appellant—13 years, 10 months, and 2 weeks old—was charged with possession of heroin with intent to distribute. The city circuit court found him delinquent.

4. The common law rule was that children below seven did not have the capacity to form criminal intent, children above fourteen had full capacity, and those in between fell on a spectrum in which the presumption of criminal capacity is rebuttable.

5. Early juvenile courts did not allow the infancy defense because the courts were purely rehabilitative and did not take moral blameworthiness into account. The recent shift towards punishment required juvenile courts to take blameworthiness into account. The infancy defense is therefore now available.

6. The state was required to prove the capacity to form criminal intent. According to the common law rule, the defendant had a 98.2% capacity to form criminal intent. Moreover, he showed clear awareness that what he was doing was wrong by trying to conceal it.

7. The court held that the state successfully overcame "the slight residual weight of the presumption of incapacity due to infancy."[98]

---

[97] Casebook p. 673.
[98] Casebook p. 678.

§ 7 Inchoate Offenses

7.1 Overview

1. **Attempt**, **solicitation**, and **conspiracy** consist of conduct meant to culminate in a substantive offense but has failed or not yet culminated.

2. Rationales for punishing inchoate crimes:

   (a) General deterrence.

   (b) Specific deterrence: those engaged in inchoate criminal activity have demonstrated their criminal proclivities.

   (c) Prevention of the target offense.

   (d) Restore balance to society.

   (e) Because those who plan to engage in criminal activity are morally blameworthy, even if they don't actually achieve their criminal ends.

3. Most jurisdictions treat inchoate offenses as distinct from the crimes toward which they tend.

4. This category of offenses relies heavily on judicial and law enforcement discretion.

5. Inchoate offense law aims to protect innocent conduct while preventing crimes in progress.

7.2 Merger and Abandonment

See attachments/inchoate-offenses.pdf.

7.3 Attempt

1. Attempt occurs when a person, with the intent to commit an offense, performs an act in furtherance of that offense.

2. **Incomplete attempt**: an actor does some of the intended acts and then stops or an extraneous factor stops her.

3. **Complete attempt**: an actor does everything she planned but is unsuccessful.

4. **Attempt is a specific intent crime.** You must have the intent to complete the target offense. Therefore, **you cannot attempt unintentional acts or conduct**—e.g., there can be no attempted involuntary manslaughter or attempted reckless murder. Most jurisdictions also **do not recognize attempted felony-murder** because attempt is a specific intent crime and specific intent to kill is not an element of felony murder.

5. Common law: attempt is a lesser offense than the target crime and is punished less harshly.

6. MPC § 5.05: inchoate offenses (including attempt) are punished at the same level as the target offense, except for capital crimes and first-degree felonies.

7. You cannot attempt to be an accomplice because accomplice liability is a form of derivative liability, not a crime.

8. With **conduct crimes** (e.g., possession or drunk driving), a person is not guilty of attempt unless he acts with specific intent to cause the unlawful result.

9. With **results crimes**, a person can be held liable if intentionally committed the actus reus of the target crime with the mens rea for the target crime.

10. MPC § 5.01 (Murray's summary): a person is guilty of attempt if, acting with the culpability required for the target offense, he:

    - (a) Deals with completed attempts of conduct offenses.
    - (b) Deals with completed attempts of results offenses.
    - (c) Deals with incomplete attempts.

11. Common law attempt tests (from Murray):

    (a) **First step test**: Once it is clear that the defendant has the purpose to commit a crime, anything the defendant does that could lead to the completion of the crime would be a sufficient actus reus to make the defendant guilty of attempt.

    (b) **Last step test**: Where the actor has done all that is in his power to do before he is prevented from committing the act by some intervention. Reflects the common law view that defendant was not guilty unless he had done all he could to commit a crime, but only failed because of bad luck.

    (c) **Physical proximity test**: Defendant is responsible for the attempt if he is in a position of physical proximity that would enable him to complete the target offense.

    (d) **Dangerous proximity test**: An attempt occurs when the defendant's conduct is in "dangerous proximity to success," or when an act "is so near to the result" that the danger of success is very great.

    　　i. How many steps towards the commission of the crime the defendant has taken?

    　　ii. How much more action is required for completion?

    　　iii. Why was the crime not completed?

7 INCHOATE OFFENSES

      iv. The amount of harm likely to result from crime.

      v. Seriousness of prospective harm; and

      vi. Appropriateness of law enforcement's interference with defendant's acts.

  (e) **Indispensable element test**: Considers whether the actor has performed an act—or obtained control over something—that is indispensable to the commission of the target offense.

  (f) **Probable desistance test**: When, in the ordinary course of events, without interruption from an external source, the actor reached a point where it was unlikely that he would have voluntarily desisted from his effort to commit the crime. The test is not concerned with how much needs to be done to commit the crime, but rather, how much has already been done. Requires the jury to think like a criminal and determine when an ordinary person in the defendant's shoes would have done enough that he would not be able to desist.

  (g) **Abnormal step test**: An attempt is a step towards crime that goes beyond the point where the normal citizen would think better of his conduct and desist. Requires the jury to think about what the normal citizen (i.e. the reasonable person, or the ordinary person) would in the defendant's circumstances.

  (h) *Res ipsa loquitur*/**unequivocality test**: An attempt occurs when a person's conduct, standing alone, unambiguously manifests his criminal intent. Considers whether the defendant's actions, viewed in the abstract, demonstrate an unequivocal intent to commit a crime.

12. MPC vs. common law:

  (a) Common law focuses on what is left to be completed.

  (b) MPC focuses on the actor's criminal disposition and considers what has already been done in furtherance of the crime.

  (c) The MPC imposes liability when there is firm evidence of criminal intent, i.e., when the defendant has taken a substantial step towards the completion of the offense. §§ 5.01(2)(a)–(g) identify scenarios that are strongly corroborative of criminal purpose.

13. **Legal and factual impossibility**: see *Thousand* below.

7.3.1 General principles

7.3.1.1 Robbins, "Double Inchoate Crimes"

1. Many jurisdictions have a few specific attempt rules alongside a general attempt statute.

2. Purpose is not deterrence but rather to give law enforcement a basis for intervention.

3. There are two varieties of criminal attempt:

    (a) **Incomplete**: Actor is interrupted.

    (b) **Complete**: Actor does every act planned but fails to cause the intended result (e.g., shoots and misses).

4. If the basis for attempt law is to support law enforcement intervention, what is the basis for punishing completed attempts?

5. Do attempts cause social harm?

7.3.1.2 Ashworth, "Criminal Attempts and the Role of Resulting Harm under the Code, and in the Common Law"

1. Prevention is the main reason for punishing preliminary steps on the way to causing harm.

2. Justifications for punishing attempt:

    (a) Retributivism: it tends to "restore an order of fairness."[99] **Harm-based** retributivism is inapplicable unless the definition of harm is broadened to include a presumed apprehension of fear of attempters. **Intent-based** retributivism holds individuals liable for their intentions, and **belief-based** retributivism for their belief that what they were doing was wrong.

    (b) Utilitarianism: incapacitation, specific deterrence, and sometimes rehabilitation.

3. Justifications for punishing the perpetrator of the completed offense:

    (a) Harm-based retributivism: the apprehension of fear can provide a basis for punishment.

    (b) Intent-based retributivism: "no relevant moral difference" between a completed attempt and a successful crime.[100]

    (c) Consequentialism: the effect of punishment must outweigh its consequences. Complete attempters show clear propensities for causing harm, so punishment is called for.

4. George Fletcher's "two patterns of criminality":[101]

    (a) "Objectivist": an act is criminal if a neutral third party could recognize the criminality of the actor's conduct.

    (b) "Subjectivist": the actor's intentions create criminality.

---

[99] Casebook p. 734.
[100] Casebook p. 735.
[101] Casebook p. 736.

7.3.1.3 ALI Comment to MPC § 5.05

1. Should attempts be treated as lesser offenses than successfully completed crimes?

2. One common law formula fixed the punishment for attempt at half of the maximum for the completed crime, or 10–50 years for crimes punishable by death or life in prison.

3. Traditionally, criminal attempts were punished less severely than completed offenses, even if the only difference was bad luck. "...the reward for failing, no matter how hard you try to succeed or how close you come, is lesser punishment."[102]

4. MPC: punishment for attempt, solicitation, and conspiracy is determined "by the gravity of the most serious offense that is its object." The completion or failure of the plan shouldn't matter because there is little deterrent force.

5. Should an attempt be treated as a less serious offense than the target crime?

7.3.2 Mens Rea

7.3.2.1 Attempted Murder and Intent: *People v. Gentry*

Since murder is a specific intent crime that requires intent to kill, attempted murder also requires intent.

1. Gentry had spilled or poured gasoline on his girlfriend which then accidentally ignited. The jury convicted him of attempted murder.

2. The jury instructions included all four culpable mental states as possible components of murder. Gentry argued on appeal that murder requires specific intent.

3. The appellate court agreed, holding that both attempted murder and murder require specific intent to kill. Knowledge is insufficient. Reversed.

4. Criminal law involves two "intents": intentional conduct and intent to commit the completed offense. They often merge, but they would be separate if, for instance, an actor shot a gun merely to scare the victim but accidentally killed him. Both intents must be proven.[103]

5. Dressler on applying MPC § 5.01:[104]

    (a) Was it a complete or incomplete attempt?

---

[102]Sanford H. Kadish, Casebook p. 737.
[103]Casebook p. 740.
[104]Casebook p. 741 n. 4.

(b) Was the target crime an offense (e.g., murder) or conduct (e.g., drunk driving) crime?

(c) 1(a) and 1(b) apply to complete attempts. 1(c) applies to complete attempts.

7.3.2.2 Attempted Felony Murder: *Bruce v. State*

Felony murder requires no specific intent to kill. Thus, there can be no attempted felony murder. Unless you live in Florida.

1. Bruce entered the victim's shoe store with a loaded gun and demanded money from the cash register. The victim ducked out of the way and Bruce shot him, causing injury but not death.

2. The trial court convicted Bruce of attempted first degree felony murder.

3. The appellate court held that criminal attempt requires specific intent to commit a particular offense. Felony murder, however, requires no specific intent to kill. Thus, there can be no attempted felony murder. Reversed.

4. (Most states agree, but Florida does not.[105])

5. Can you be guilty of attempted statutory rape? Under the MPC the answer is yes. **To be guilty of attempt, the actor must have acted with the mental state required for the target offense.** Statutory rape is a strict liability offense, i.e., no particular mental state is required. Since mistake of age is irrelevant for the target offense, it is likewise irrelevant for the attempt.[106]

7.3.3 Actus Reus

7.3.3.1 *United States v. Mandujano*

Attempting to define attempt. See also the list of common law attempt tests at the top of this section.

1. *United States v. Noreikis*: the distinction between preparation and attempt "is one incapable of being formulated into a hard and fast rule."[107]

2. *United States v. Coplon*: attempt is when "he has done all that it is within his power to do, but has been prevented by intervention from outside" (Learned Hand).

    (a) *Locus poenitentiae*: "place of repentance."

---
[105]Casebook p. 743.
[106]Casebook p. 745.
[107]Casebook p. 746.

7 INCHOATE OFFENSES

3. *Mims v. United States*, relying on a test from *People v. Buffum*: an "appreciable fragment" must have been committed, it must be in progress such that it will be completed unless interrupted, and it must not be equivocal.

4. Others (from the case notes):

    (a) *United States v. Oviedo*: attempt exist if the objective acts, "without any reliance on the *mens rea*, mark the defendant's conduct as criminal in nature."[108]

    (b) *Stokes v. State*: if the "design of a person to commit a crime is clearly shown, slight acts done in furtherance of this design will constitute an attempt."

    (c) *People v. Luna*: if intent is "clearly shown," any act toward commission constitutes attempt.

    (d) Sayre, "Criminal Attempts": the more serious the crime, the "further back" in the series of preliminary acts should the law look for acts constituting attempt.

    (e) Enker, "Impossibility in Criminal Attempts—Legality and the Legal Process": courts must weigh several factors, including (1) whether the act is "sufficiently close to the substantive crime," (2) whether the actor's conduct makes one "reasonably certain that he is firmly committed to a specific illegal venture," and (3) whether "the act is sufficiently unambiguous to demonstrate the actor's illegal intent."[109]

7.3.3.2 Locus Poenitentiae: *Commonwealth v. Peaslee*

Preparation becomes attempt if it "comes very near" to the completed act.

1. The defendant had prepared to burn down a building. He asked one of employees to start the fire, and the employee refused. Later, the two of them drove toward the building to be burned, but turned back a quarter of a mile away.

2. The question was whether the defendant's actions "near enough to the accomplishment of the substantive offense to be punishable."[110]

3. If preparation "comes very near" to the completed act, it can be punished as attempt. But in this case, preparation to set the fire without any intent to actually light it is "too remote."

---

[108] Casebook p. 747.
[109] Casebook p. 748.
[110] Casebook p. 750.

7.3.3.3 No Chance of Success: *People v. Rizzo*

There can be no attempt if there is no chance of success.

1. The defendant and three others drove around looking for a man they intended to rob. When the defendant jumped out of the car to look for the man, all four were arrested. It turned out that the person they intended to rob was nowhere nearby.

2. The court held that there cannot be an attempt if there is no chance of success. "...these defendants had planned to commit a crime and were looking around the city for an opportunity to commit it, but the opportunity fortunately never came."[111]

7.3.3.4 *People v. Miller*

With clear intent, any slight act done in furtherance of the target offense constitutes attempt.

1. The defendant had earlier threatened to kill Albert Jeans. Later that day, he went, carrying a loaded rifle, to a field where Jeans and the constable were planting hops. He surrendered his gun to the constable.

2. The court cited *Stokes*, which held that with clear intent, any slight act done in furtherance constitutes attempt. But the *Stokes* test, the court held, "still presupposes some direct act or movement in the execution of the design."[112] As long as the actor remains equivocal, there can be no attempt.

7.3.3.5 Preparation and Substantial Steps: *State v. Reeves*

An actor is guilty of attempt if she takes substantial steps towards the completed offense.

1. Two twelve-year-old girls decided to kill their teacher with rat poison. The teacher saw the girls standing over her desk and giggling. The school found rat poison in one of their purses.

2. The trial court found them guilty of attempted second-degree murder.

3. The current Tennessee statute, based on the MPC, finds attempt if the "conduct constitutes a substantial step toward the commission of the offense."[113]

---

[111]Casebook p. 754.
[112]Casebook p. 756.
[113]Casebook p. 760.

7 INCHOATE OFFENSES

4. The defendant argued that the state deliberately omitted the examples in MPC § 510.2 of conduct that are strongly corroborative of the actor's criminal intent. However, the court was not convinced that this omission meant that the legislature intended to retain the sharp distinction between "mere preparation" and the "act itself." It held that the jury is free to apply the MPC's "substantial step" rule.

7.3.4 Special defenses

7.3.5 Impossibility: *People v. Thousand*

1. Thousand sent lewd pictures to someone he thought was an underage girl but who turned out to be an undercover cop. He was charged with attempted distribution of obscene material to a minor.

2. Thousand argued that the existence of a child was a required element of the offense and he moved for dismissal. The trial court granted the motion and the appellate court affirmed.

3. **Factual impossibility**: the defendant intends to commit a crime but fails because of a factual circumstance unknown to her or beyond her control—e.g., trying to kill someone by pulling the trigger of an unloaded gun. Never recognized as a defense.

4. **Pure legal impossibility**: criminal law does not prohibit the actor's conduct or intended result—e.g., a man has sex with a fifteen-year-old believing that the statutory rape law sets the minimum age at sixteen, but in fact sets it at fifteen. He would not be found guilty.

5. **Hybrid legal impossibility**: the actor's goal was illegal but he could not complete it because of a factual mistake regarding the legal status of a relevant factor—e.g., shooting a corpse believing it is alive.

6. Any instance of hybrid legal impossibility can be redrawn as factual impossibility and is therefore not available as a defense in most jurisdictions.

7. The court here declined to accept factual impossibility or hybrid legal impossibility as defenses. Reversed.

7.3.6 Abandonment: *Commonwealth v. McCloskey*

Abandonment is a defense to attempt. It is distinct from failing to complete the attempt.

1. The defendant prepared to escape from prison. He began to escape, including cutting barbed wire, but changed his mind.

2. The trial court found him guilty of attempted prison breach.

3. The Supreme Court of Pennsylvania reversed on the grounds that the defendant had "not yet attempted the act."[114]

4. Judge Cercone, concurring, agreed with the outcome, but argued that the basis should be the defense of **abandonment**. Otherwise, the prison guards would not have been able to stop the defendant's escape until he was scaling the prison walls.

    (a) The PA legislature substantially adopted the MPC, including § 5.01. He argued that the court had long ago adopted abandonment as an affirmative defense. And if it hadn't, it should have.[115]

7.4 Assault

1. Under common law, mayhem consisted of injury "impairing the victim's ability to defend himself or to annoy his adversary."[116]

2. Battery: any offensive and unlawful contact.

3. Assault was **originally just the attempt to commit battery**. It required stricter proximity than ordinary attempt. It evolved to include menacing and actual attempts, as well as conditional assaults (i.e., threats).

4. The MPC removed the common law categories and implemented a single definition under § 211.1. It consolidates assault and battery and removes the increased proximity requirement.

7.5 Solicitation

1. Solicitation is the **asking, enticing, inducing, or counseling of another to commit a crime**. Under the common law approach, the target offense must have been a felony or a serious misdemeanor.

2. MPC § 5.02: "A person is guilty of solicitation to commit a crime if with the purpose of promoting or facilitating its commission he commands, encourages or requests another person to engage in specific conduct that would constitute such crime or an attempt to commit such crime or which would establish his complicity in its commission or attempted commission."

3. MPC differences from common law:

    (a) Applies to all crimes (not just felonies or misdemeanors).

    (b) Possible to solicit an attempt, knowing the crime cannot be completed.

---

[114] Casebook p. 787.
[115] Casebook p. 788.
[116] Casebook p. 790.

7 INCHOATE OFFENSES

(c) Possible to solicit complicity (e.g., providing a gun so A can kill B, which is not solicitation at common law because there was no request to commit a substantive offense.)

(d) Uncommunicated solicitation is still solicitation. *Cotton*.

7.5.1 Defining Solicitation: *State v. Mann*

1. "Solicitation involves the asking, enticing, inducing, or counselling of another to commit a crime."[117]

2. "...the solicitor is morally more culpable than a conspirator..."

3. *Merger*: "The offense of solicitation merges into the crime solicited if the latter attempt is committed or attempted by the solicited party."[118]

7.5.2 Completed Communication: *State v. Cotton*

The MPC criminalizes solicitations that fail to reach the intended recipient, but New Mexico does not recognize this provision.

1. While in prison, the defendant wrote letters to his wife asking her to help prevent his step-daughter from testifying against him. His cellmate covertly removed the letters from their envelopes and turned them over to the authorities.

2. The defendant was convicted of two counts of criminal solicitation.

3. The appellate court noted that the New Mexico state legislature explicitly omitted MPC § 5.02(2), which criminalizes solicitations that fail to reach the intended recipient. The court reasoned that this omission indicates the legislature's intent to require actual communication for solicitation to be accomplished.

4. Reversed.

7.6 Conspiracy

1. At common law, a conspiracy was a mutual agreement or understanding, express or implied, between two or more persons to commit a criminal act or to accomplish a legal act by unlawful means. Modernly, jurisdictions define a conspiracy as a **(1) mutual agreement or understanding, express or implied, (2) between two or more persons (3) to commit a criminal act.**

2. The MPC requires **proof of an overt act** toward the target offense, unless the target offense is a first- or second-degree felony. § 5.03(5).

---

[117]Casebook p. 792.
[118]Casebook p. 793.

7 INCHOATE OFFENSES

3. Agreement must be proven by inference and circumstantial evidence.

4. Conspiracy involves (1) intent to form an agreement and (2) intent to commit the elements of the target offense.

5. Under the common law, conspiracy **does not merge** into the completed offense. Under the MPC, conspiracy *does* merge.

6. **Pinkerton liability** holds each conspirator liable for the criminal acts of any co-conspirator. There is **no Pinkerton liability in the MPC**, thought most jurisdictions where the MPC has influence have retained Pinkerton liability. [119]).

7. Conspiracy is a **specific intent crime**. The prosecution must prove intent to join the agreement—e.g., you cannot accidentally join a conspiracy.

8. Circumstances can, however, are sometimes sufficient to prove that the defendant's knowledge of the criminal activity demonstrates his intent to participate (see *Lauria* below):

    (a) When the purveyor of legal goods for illegal uses has acquired a stake in the criminal venture.

    (b) When no legitimate use for the goods or services exists.

    (c) When the volume of business with the buyer is grossly disproportionate to any legitimate demand.

    (d) Under the MPC, there is no conspiracy where a provider of goods or services is aware of the criminal activity but does not share the criminal purpose.

9. Common law factors from which intent can be inferred: association, knowledge, presence, participation.[120]

10. Most jurisdictions follow the common law for conspiracy, not the MPC.

11. MPC vs. common law:

    (a) The MPC allows unilateral conspiracies ("conspiracies of one").[121]

    (b) **Scope of conspiracy** (Murray): Under the MPC, If a person guilty of conspiracy under § 5.03(1) knows that a person with whom he conspires to commit a crime has conspired with another person or persons to commit the same crime, he is guilty of conspiring with such other person or persons, whether or not he knows their identity, to commit such crime.[122]

---

[119] "Law would lose all sense of just proportion if simply because of the conspiracy itself each [conspirator] were held accountable for thousands of additional offenses of which he was completely unaware and which he did not influence at all" ALI commentary to MPC § 2.06.

[120] Casebook p. 818.

[121] MPC § 5.03(1).

[122] § 5.03(2).

12. Prosecutors love conspiracies. Learned Hand: conspiracy is the "darling of the modern prosecutor's nursery."[123] Murray:

   (a) Separate crime with its own penalties

   (b) Allows apprehension of the defendant at an earlier stage than attempt.

   (c) As we will discuss, members of a conspiracy are vicariously liable for the acts of their co-conspirators in furtherance of the conspiracy.

   (d) Allows for the apprehension and prosecution of large groups of individuals

   (e) Conspiracy is a continuing offense, which gives prosecutors a long time in which to file charges.

   (f) Prosecutors may file charges for conspiracy in any venue where an act of the conspiracy occurred.

   (g) Evidentiary exceptions permit the admissibility of co-conspirator's statements.

   (h) Under federal law, conspiracy aggravates the degree of the target offense.

13. **Multiple crimes** under the MPC (Murray):If a person conspires to commit a number of crimes, he is guilty of only one conspiracy so long as such multiple crimes are the object of the same agreement or continuous conspiratorial relationship.

14. **Wheel conspiracy**: the spokes do not know each other, but they are all connected to a central hub. A shared interest connects them through the "rim." A wheel conspiracy is not complete unless there is the rim. See *Kilgore* below, and *Kotteakos*, where the Supreme Court held that small conspiracies could not be shown to be a larger conspiracy unless the spokes shared a common interest—e.g., if the individual borrowers used part of the proceeds obtained by the others' loans as the down payments for their loans.

15. **Chain conspiracy**: several layers of personnel. Their individual success depends on the success of the entire chain.

7.6.1 General Principles

7.6.1.1 Drug Smuggling: Kerman, *Orange is the New Black: My Year in a Women's Prison*

1. Kerman was indicted on conspiracy charges for drug smuggling and money laundering. She pleaded guilty and received a 30-month sentence.

2. She was liable for the entire scope of the conspiracy.

---
[123]*Harrison v. United States* in *Understanding Criminal Law* p. 422.

7.6.1.2 People v. Carter

1. "'The gist of the offense of criminal conspiracy lies in the unlawful agreement.' The crime is complete upon the formation of the agreement..."[124]

2. Some jurisdictions require an overt act, but the threshold is low.

3. **The specific intent is twofold: (1) intent to combine with others and (2) intent to accomplish the illegal objective.**

4. Conspiracy fills the gap created when attempt is too narrowly conceived.

5. Often used to fight organized crime.

6. "...collective criminal agreement—partnership in crime—presents a greater potential threat to the public than individual delicts."[125]

7. The *Callahan* court argued that conspiratorial groups are dangerous because they can lead to criminal activity beyond the original intended crime. Others have argued that conspiracies are less dangerous because plans are more likely to leak or that some conspirators' doubts will influence other participants.

8. Katyal: groups polarize toward extremes and are thus more dangerous.[126]

9. Acts that are immoral but not criminal can be punished with conspiracy charges.[127]

10. Spectrum of inchoate offenses: solicitation <conspiracy >attempt.

11. Is "attempted conspiracy" cognizable or is it the same as solicitation?

7.6.1.3 Pinkerton Liability: *Pinkerton v. United States*

Pinkerton liability holds each conspirator liable for the criminal acts of any co-conspirator.

1. Two brothers were found guilty of conspiracy and multiple substantive counts of violating the Internal Revenue Code. Daniel did not participate in the substantive crimes. The question is whether participation in the conspiracy is enough to find the conspirator guilty of the substantive crimes.

2. Daniel argued that direct participation was necessary to find guilt on the substantive counts.

---

[124] Casebook p. 797.
[125] Casebook p. 798.
[126] Casebook p. 799.
[127] Casebook p. 799–800.

7 INCHOATE OFFENSES

3. The Supreme Court disagreed, holding that "an overt act of one partner may be the act of all without any new agreement specifically directed to that act."[128]

4. Judge Rutledge, dissenting: such vicarious liability is appropriate in civil but not criminal contexts. He finds it "dangerous" but does not explain why.

7.6.2 Mens rea

7.6.2.1 Conspiracy to Commit Implied Malice Murder: *People v. Swain*

It is not possible to conspire to commit a crime that does not require specific intent.

1. Swain and Chatman were both convicted of conspiracy to commit murder and other crimes "stemming from the drive-by shooting death of a 15-year-old boy."[129]

2. In jail, Swain boasted about being a good shot. But at trial, he testified that he was not in the van at the time of the shooting.

3. Chatman claimed the original plan was to steal the decedent's car. He claimed he fired shots in self defense.

4. The jury found Chatman guilty of second-degree murder and conspiracy. It found Swain guilty of conspiracy but not murder.

5. The question on appeal was whether conspiracy to commit murder requires express malice or whether it is possible to conspire to commit implied malice murder. Implied malice murder does not require an intent to kill.

6. California recognizes three kinds of second-degree murder:[130]

    (a) Unpremeditated with express malice.
    (b) Implied malice (i.e., depraved heart).
    (c) Felony murder.

7. The charge here was implied malice murder, which does not require a specific intent to kill.

8. Conspiracy requires specific intent to commit the elements of the target crime, it is not possible to conspire to commit a crime that does not require specific intent.

9. Reversed.

---

[128]Casebook p. 802.
[129]Casebook p. 806.
[130]Casebook p. 808.

7.6.2.2 Suppliers as Conspirators: *People v. Lauria*

A suppliers of goods can be held liable as a conspirator (1) when he overtly intends to participate in criminal activity, or (2) when intent can be inferred on (a) his interest in the activity or (b) the seriousness of the crime.

1. Lauria operated an answering service. He knew many of his customers used it for prostitution.

2. Lauria was indicted for conspiracy to commit prostitution. The trial court set aside the indictment for lack of "reasonable or probable cause."[131]

3. The appellate court asked, "[u]nder what circumstances does a supplier become part of a conspiracy to further an illegal enterprise by furnishing goods or services which he knows are to be used by the buyer for criminal purposes?"[132]

4. Two Supreme Court cases addressed this question:

    (a) *Falcone*: a seller of sugar, yeast, and cans was not guilty in a moonshining conspiracy, even though it knew of the criminal activity.

    (b) *Direct Sales*: a morphine distributor was found guilty of conspiracy for selling 300 times the normal requirement of the drug to a physician.

    (c) The rule is that intent to "further, promote, and cooperate" in the criminal activity must be present for the actor to be guilty of conspiracy.

5. The appellate court identified three areas where intent can be inferred:

    (a) When the seller of goods has a stake in the criminal activity (e.g., renting a room at inflated prices to a prostitute).

    (b) When there is no legitimate use for the goods or services (e.g., supplying horse-racing information by wire).

    (c) When the volume of business with the buyer is "grossly disproportionate to any legitimate demand."

6. The court developed a two-part rule for establishing the intent of a supplier: (1) when he overtly intends to participate in criminal activity, or (2) when intent can be inferred on (a) his interest in the activity or (b) the seriousness of the crime.[133]

7. Inferences of intent do not apply to misdemeanors.

8. The conspiracy charges against Lauria do not stand because he was only charged with furthering a misdemeanor.

---

[131] Casebook p. 810.
[132] Casebook p. 810.
[133] Casebook p. 813.

7 INCHOATE OFFENSES

7.6.3 Actus Reus

7.6.3.1 Goldstein, "Conspiracy to Defraud the United States"

1. The conspiratorial agreement is a "theoretical construct." By calling it an act, "courts foster the already elaborate illusion that conspiracy reaches actual, not potential, harm."[134]

2. Juries can find conspiracy "on less evidence than might otherwise be required."

7.6.3.2 Inferring Conspiracy: *Commonwealth v. Azim*

Conspiracy can be established by inference.

1. Azim was carrying two men in his car. He stopped the car for them to assault and rob another man. He was convicted of assault, robbery, and conspiracy.

2. On appeal, Azim argued that "because his conspiracy conviction was not supported by sufficient evidence against him, the charges of assault and robbery must also fail."[135]

3. In *Volk*, the court held that conspiracy could "be inferentially established"—i.e., the agreement need not be explicit.

4. The court held that there was sufficient evidence of conspiracy, and because conspiracy was established, Azim was also guilty of the criminal acts of his co-conspirators.

7.6.3.3 *Commonwealth v. Cook*

Conspiracy can also be difficult to establish by inference. Cf. *Azim*, above, which is difficult to reconcile with this case.

1. Cook was convicted of conspiracy to commit rape. On appeal, he argued that there was insufficient evidence to establish a conspiracy.

2. The victim visited a housing project to visit her boyfriend, who turned out not to be home. The defendant and his brother invited her to hang out on their porch. After forty-five minutes, Cook's brother suggested that the three of them go to a convenience store to buy cigarettes. On a path along the way, the victim slipped, and Cook's brother raped her.

3. The Court found no conspiracy because there was no evidence of a preconceived plan, the conduct up to the crime was in the open, and the criminal action was spontaneous.

---
[134]Casebook p. 816.
[135]Casebook p. 818.

7 INCHOATE OFFENSES

4. The Court also rejected the Commonwealth's argument that Cook's complicity as an accomplice made him a co-conspirator. There was no prior agreement to commit a criminal act.

5. Reversed.

7.6.4 Scope of the Agreement

7.6.4.1 ALI Commentary to MPC § 5.03

1. **"The scope problem"**: "Has a retailer conspired with the smugglers to import the narcotics? Has a prostitute conspired with the leaders of the vice ring to commit the acts of prostitution of each other prostitute who is controlled by the ring?"

7.6.4.2 Wheel and Chain Conspiracies: *Kilgore v. State*

A wheel conspiracy requires multiple "spokes" from a "hub" with a "rim" connecting the spokes.

1. Facts:

2. February 6, 1981: David Oldaker and Greg Benton attempted to kill Roger Norman at the request of Tom Harden.

3. June 8, 1981: Kilgore (the defendant) and Lee Berry allegedly shot Norman in the back while he was driving but did not kill him.

4. July 8, 1981: Kilgore and Bob Price allegedly successfully killed Norman. Tom Carden allegedly had given them money.

5. Kilgore was convicted of murder.

6. At trial, Oldaker testified that Benton told him that the man who wanted Norman killed was Tom Carden. The Supreme Court of Georgia found that this testimony was admissible only if Oldaker, Benton, and Kilgore were co-conspirators. This was a "wheel" conspiracy in which Tom Carden communicated with each of the "spokes" individually—however, there was no evidence suggesting that Oldaker and Benton had any contact with Kilgore. Thus, the three were not co-conspirators and Oldaker's testimony was inadmissible.

7. (It's not clear whether the court upheld the conviction after it determined that the testimony was inadmissible hearsay.)

7.6.4.3 Single Agreement, Multiple Offenses: *Braverman v. United States*

A single agreement can only be punished as a single conspiracy, even if it aimed at several criminal offenses.

1. Defendant moonshiners were indicted on seven counts of conspiracy to violate U.S. internal revenue laws. The defendants moved to require the government to choose one of the seven counts, arguing that the evidence could not prove seven different conspiracies. The government argued that the indictment was proper because there were seven different criminal goals of a single ongoing conspiracy.

2. The jury returned a guilty verdict on each of the seven counts. The Sixth Circuit affirmed.

3. The government conceded that there was a single agreement among the conspirators. The Supreme Court held that a single agreement can only be punished as a single conspiracy, even if it aimed at several criminal offenses. Reversed.

7.6.5 Defenses

7.6.5.1 Wharton's Rule: *Ianelli v. United States*

Wharton's Rule prevents conspiracy charges for crimes requiring multiple participants. Wharton's rule presumes merger.

1. The eight petitioners were convicted of conspiring to violate and violating a federal gambling statute which criminalized gambling businesses involving at least five people.[136]

2. The Third Circuit affirmed.

3. "Wharton's Rule" prevents conspiracy charges for crimes requiring multiple participants.[137] The classic "Wharton's Rule" offenses are adultery, incest, bigamy, and duelling.[138]

4. Courts were divided on whether the rule requires the conspiracy charge to be dismissed before trial or whether a prosecutor can charge both and instruct the jury that conviction for the offense precludes conviction for the conspiracy.

5. Courts were also divided on whether Wharton's Rule applies when there are more people involved than are necessary to commit the offense.

---

[136] 18 U.S.C. § 1955.
[137] Casebook p. 839.
[138] Casebook p. 841.

7 INCHOATE OFFENSES

6. **The MPC does not recognize Wharton's Rule.**

7. One exception exists for when the two conspirators are not the two who will commit the crime (e.g., "go commit adultery with my wife"). In those cases, Wharton's Rule does not apply.

8. Wharton's Rule was intended to apply to offenses that "require concerted criminal activity... absent legislative intent to the contrary, the Rule supports a presumption that the two merge when the substantive offense is proved."[139] Here, however, the legislative history of the gambling statute shows a clear intent to target organized crime, so it makes sense not to merge the conspiracy and the substantive offense.

7.6.5.2 Gebardi v. United States

Under the common law, acquiescence to activity in which acquiescence does not estasblish guilt is insufficient to establish conspiracy for either conspirator. Under the MPC, conspiracy can be unilateral.

1. Gebardi was convicted of conspiracy to violate the Mann Act (transporting "any woman or girl for the purpose of prostitution or debauchery, or for any other immoral purpose"[140]).

2. The Mann Act requires more than the woman's "mere acquiescence." She must "aid or assist" her own transport. The **"legislative exemption defense"** holds that a victim cannot be guilty of contributing to her own victimization. **Victims cannot be co-conspirators.**

3. "As there is no proof that the man conspired with anyone else to bring about the transportation, the convictions of both petitioners [for conspiracy] must be reversed."[141]

4. (Under MPC § 5.04(1), the court would likely find the man guilty of conspiracy.)

7.6.5.3 Withdrawal from Conspiracy: *People v. Sconce*

1. Sconce offered Garcia $10,000 to kill Estephan. Garcia offered $5,000 to Dutton to perform the killing. Three weeks later, Sconce told Garcia to call it off. Meanwhile, Dutton had been arrested on a parole violation.

2. The trial court set aside the information relating to conspiracy because Sconce had withdrawn.

---

[139] Casebook p. 842.
[140] Casebook p. 844
[141] Casebook p. 845.

3. The appellate court held that withdrawal is a complete defense to conspiracy only if it occurs before an overt act. Here, Sconce had already completed the conspiracy, and the overt act was giving the money, so his withdrawal only precluded liability for future acts of his co-conspirators.

4. "...withdrawal from the conspiracy is not a defense to the completed crime of conspiracy..."[142]

5. Reversed.

---

[142] Casebook p. 847.

§ 8 Accomplice Liability

1. An accomplice is liable for the principal's crimes if the accomplice intentionally assists the principal in committing the criminal conduct.

2. **Accomplice liability is not a substantive offense** on its own. Rather, accomplice liability is a theory of **derivative liability**.

3. Accomplices are prosecuted for the principal's crime.

4. MPC accomplice liability is in § 2.06.

5. Can knowledge of a crime establish intent to aid its commission?

    (a) The majority view is **no**. Complicity requires participation. There must be a "community of purpose."

    (b) The MPC also requires purpose to encourage the substantive offense. Knowledge is insufficient.

    (c) A person is not an accomplice unless he shares the criminal intent of the principal.

6. **Conduct**: Accomplice liability requires that the person intended to promote the principal's *conduct*, but not necessarily the end *result*. See *Riley* below.

7. Under both the common law majority view and the MPC, you can be liable as an accomplice for the consequences of unintentional acts, so long as the act of assistance was **undertaken with the same level of culpability as required for the underlying offense**. I.e., an accomplice can be liable if she acts with the **same mental state as the principal**—e.g., if a taxi passenger negligently encourages the driver to drive negligently and he causes an accident, she is liable. But if he drives recklessly, she is not liable.

8. Under old common law rules, accomplice liability was entirely tied to the success of the principal. The accomplice could only be convicted if the principal was convicted. Now, the defendant can still be convicted as an accomplice, as long as *a* principal committed the crime.

9. **Justification and excuse**: If the principal is acquitted on an *excuse* defense, the accomplice can still be liable. If the principal is acquitted on a *justification*, there has been no crime and there is no basis for accomplice liability. See *Lopez* below.

10. **Legislative exemption**: "Where the Legislature has dealt with crimes which necessarily involve the joint action of two or more persons, and where no punishment at all is provided for the conduct, or misconduct, of one of the participants, the party whose participation is not denounced by

8 ACCOMPLICE LIABILITY

statute cannot be charged with criminal conduct on either a conspiracy or aiding and abetting theory." I.e., a victim cannot aid the commission of the crime that victimizes him. MPC § 2.06(6)(a) is in accord. See *Megan R.* below.

11. **Abandonment**:

    (a) Common law: an accomplice can abandon the criminal enterprise, but he "must communicate his withdrawal to the principal and make bona fide efforts to neutralize the effect of his prior assistance."[143]

    (b) MPC: a person is not an accomplice if he "(1) terminates his assistsance, (2) gives timely warning to the police of the impending offense, or (3) in some other manner attempts to prevent the commission of the crime."[144]

8.1 General Principles

8.1.1 Common Law Terminology: *State v. Ward*

1. **Principal in the first degree**: one who actually commits a crime.

2. **Principal in the second degree**: one who "aided, counseled, commanded, or encouraged the commission [of the act] in his presence..."—e.g., lookout, getaway driver.[145].

3. **Accessory before the fact**: same as principal in the second degree, but not physically present—e.g., casing the bank, buying disguises.

4. **Accessory after the fact**: one who renders assistance in hindering detection, arrest, trial, or punishment.

    (a) Accessories after the fact cannot be tried before the principal is tried.

5. Modern equivalents:

    (a) **Principal** = first-degree principal.

    (b) **Accomplice** = second-degree principal or accessory before the fact. Accessories after the fact are not accomplices under the modern approach because they are less culpable, but they may be subject to liability for misprision.

---

[143] *Understanding Criminal Law* p. 484.
[144] *Understanding Criminal Law* p. 494; MPC § 2.06(6).
[145] Casebook p. 849

8.1.2 Theoretical Foundations for Derivative Liability

1. An accomplice (under common law, a principal in the second degree or an accessory before the fact) is not guilty of "aiding and abetting" but rather is **guilty of the substantive crime itself**. The "elements" (mens rea and actus reus) of an accomplice's act are convenient shorthand but not rigorously defined.

2. Themes in accomplice liability:

    (a) What makes a person an accomplice so as to justify holding that person liable for the completed crime?

    (b) Are there cases where it is possible to convict a second party of a more serious offense than the primary party?

    (c) When can an accomplice avoid liability despite participation in criminal activity?

8.1.3 *People v. Hoselton*

Aiders and abettors must share the criminal intent of the principal.

1. Hoselton was trespassing with several friends on a barge. They broke into a storage unit and stole several tools. Hoselton was unaware of his friends' intent to steal until they opened the door. He went to a car at the other end of the barge. His friends loaded the stolen goods into the car and drove him directly home.

2. Hoselton was convicted of entering without breaking a vessel with intent to commit larceny.

3. In a voluntary interview, Hoselton was asked, "Were you keeping a lookout?" and he responded, "You could say that. I just didn't want to go down in there."

4. The appellate court held that an aider and abettor (a principal in the second degree) must share the criminal intent of the principal in the first degree. It found that Hoselton's voluntary statement was insufficient to establish criminal intent.

5. Reversed.

8.1.4 Kerman, *Orange is the New Black*

1. See above, p. 55.

8.2 Mens Rea

8.2.1 *People v. Lauria*

1. See above, p. 57.

8.2.2 No Principal, and Conduct vs. Result: *Riley v. State*

Accomplice liability requires that the person intended to promote the principal's *conduct*, but not necessarily the end *result*. This accounts for cases where the principal is not identifiable.

1. Riley and Portella opened fire on an unsuspecting crowd, wounding two of them. It was not clear who fired the wounding shots.

2. The jury found Riley guilty as an accomplice.

3. In *Echols*, the Alaska appellate court held that accomplice liability requires intent to commit the target crime.

4. Here, the court reversed the *Echols* rule. It noted that the Alaska statute was based closely on MPC § 2.06. MPC § 2.06(4) indicates that an accomplice has the requisite mens rea if he acts with the culpability sufficient for the target offense. Accomplice liability requires that the person intended to promote the principal's *conduct*, but not necessarily the end *result*.[146]

5. Affirmed.

8.2.3 Natural-and-Probable Consequences Doctrine: *State v. Linscott*

An accomplice is liable for the reasonably foreseeable consequences of the criminal undertaking.

1. Linscott and several others intended to rob Grenier at his home. One of the other robbers, Fuller, fired a shot which killed Grenier.

2. At trial, Linscott argued that Fuller often carried a gun with him because he was a hunter. He argued further that he had no intent of causing a death in the course of the robbery.

3. The trial court found him guilty of robbery and, by accomplice liability, guilty of murder. Although Linscott did not intend to kill Grenier, the murder was a reasonably foreseeable consequence of the robbery.

4. The appellate court rejected Linscott's argument that the foreseeable consequence rule violated due process. Affirmed.

5. Juries must follow a four-step process in deciding whether to apply the natural-and-probable-consequences doctrine:[147]

    (a) Did the primary party commit the target offense (or an inchoate version)?

---

[146]Casebook p. 861–62.
[147]Casebook p. 866.

8 ACCOMPLICE LIABILITY

(b) Was the secondary party an accomplice?

(c) Did the primary party commit *another* crime beyond the target offense?

(d) Were the additional crimes reasonable and foreseeable consequences of the criminal acts?

(e) If the answer is yes to all of the above, the doctrine applies.

8.3 Actus Reus

8.3.1 Slackjaw Deadeye: *State v. V.T.*

Active encouragement is required to establish accomplice liability. A comforting or encouraging presence can suffice in some cases (e.g., standing lookout or providing moral support).

1. V.T., Moose, and Joey were staying at a relative's house. The relative's camcorder went missing and turned up soon after at a pawnshop. The camcorder contained a video of Moose calling a friend and discussed pawning the stolen camcorder. V.T. "never spoke or gestured during any of this footage."[148]

2. V.T. was charged with two counts of theft. The judge found him guilty of misdemeanor theft of the camcorder.

3. The appellate court held that V.T.'s passive presence alone was insufficient to establish accomplice liability. The state was required to show some kind of active encouragement. Reversed.

8.3.2 Small Encouragement: *Wilcox v. Jeffery*

Sometimes very small encouragement suffices, especially when politics are involved.

1. Wilcox ran *Jazz Illustrated* magazine. Coleman Hawkins entered the country without permission to take employment. Hawkins gave a performance that Wilcox attended and wrote about for his magazine.

2. The court found him guilty of aiding and abetting. It noted that "his presence and his payment to go there [to Hawkins's show] was an encouragement."[149]

---

[148] Casebook p. 869.
[149] Casebook p. 873.

8.4 Liability of Principals and Accomplices

8.4.1 Innocent Agency Doctrine: *Bailey v. Commonwealth*

I'm a [non-culpable] fool to do your dirty work.

1. Bailey and Murdock were drunk and taunting each other on citizens' band radio. Bailey convinced Murdock to stand on his porch with his gun. He then anonymously called the police on Murdock. Murdock opened fire. The police fired back, killing him.

2. The trial court instructed the jury that it should find Bailey guilty of involuntary manslaughter if he acted with callous disregard for human life and that he proximately caused Murdock's death. The jury convicted him.

3. The appellate court affirmed, holding that "Bailey undertook to cause Murdock harm and used the police to accomplish that purpose."[150] Murdock's firing on the police was a reasonably foreseeable intervening cause.

4. The "innocent agency doctrine" holds a defendant liable if he uses an innocent agent to commit the offense.

8.4.2 Justification: *United States v. Lopez*

If the target offense was justified then the principal did not commit a criminal act and there can be no accomplice liability.

1. McIntosh landed a helicopter in a prison to help his girlfriend, Lopez, escape. Before trial, McIntosh and Lopez indicated intent to raise a "necessity/duress" defense based on threats to Lopez's life. McIntosh requested a jury instruction that if Lopez acted under necessity/duress, McIntosh could not be guilty of aiding and abetting.[151]

2. The court held that Lopez's necessity defense was a justification, not an excuse. If the jury found Lopez not guilty, the principal would have committed no criminal act, and therefore there cannot be accomplice liability. McIntosh is entitled to his jury instruction.

8.4.3 More Serious Crime than the Principal's: *People v. McCoy*

An accomplice can be convicted of a more serious crime than the principal's crime because their mental states are distinct.

1. McCoy and Lakey were tried for first-degree murder in a drive-by shooting. McCoy shot the victim. He claimed self-defense, which the jury rejected.

---
[150]Casebook p. 882.
[151]Casebook p. 885.

2. The appellate court overturned on the ground that the jury instructions on self-defense were inadequate. It also reversed Lakey's murder conviction on the ground that an accomplice cannot be convicted of a more serious offense than the principal.

3. The California Supreme Court held that an aider and abettor's mental state is distinct from the principal's mental state and might well be more culpable (e.g., Iago and Othello). Reversed.

8.5 Limitations on Accomplice Liability

8.5.1 Aiding Your Own Victimization? *In re Megan R.*

A victim of a crime cannot be an accomplice to its commission.

1. Oscar Rodriguez and Megan R. broke into the home of Joani Rodriguez to have sex. Megan was 14 years old. The juvenile court convicted her of burglary (breaking and entering into the dwelling of another at night with the intent to commit a felony therein).

2. On appeal, Megan argued that she could not logically aid the crime of her own statutory rape.[152] The court agreed. Reversed.

8.5.2 Renunciation: *State v. Formella*

To counter complicity in a crime, an accomplice must take affirmative steps to end his involvement. Passive withdrawal is not enough.

1. Formella and friends met a group of students in a school hallway after school had dismissed. The group asked them to stand lookout while they stole math exams. While the group was away, Formella decided to abandon the project and went outside to the parking lot. Later, someone informed the school about the theft. Formella was charged and convicted of the theft based on accomplice liability.

2. Formella argued that he was not an accomplice because he ended his involvement with the crime. The relevant statute required that he would not be held liable as an accomplice if (among other requirements) "he wholly deprived his complicity of effectiveness in the commission of the crime."[153] The court held that to counter his prior complicity, Formella must have acted affirmatively. Passive withdrawal is insufficient. Affirmed.

---

[152] Cf. *Gebardi*, above, where the court found that a woman could not be found guilty as a co-conspirator to violate the Mann Act.

[153] Casebook p. 892.

www.ingramcontent.com/pod-product-compliance
Lightning Source LLC
Chambersburg PA
CBHW062222220526
45471CB00009B/3306